CONQUER

The High Achiever's Guide
To Beating Burnout

Information For All Readers

This text discusses important concepts related to your health. The work has been checked for accuracy and relevance by licensed healthcare professionals. However, you should remain aware that this text does not act as a substitute for consultation with a licensed healthcare expert who can make a proper diagnosis having regard for your unique circumstances.

Copyright © 2023 by LearnWell Books.

All rights reserved. No part of this publication may be reproduced, distributed, or transmitted in any form or by any means, including photocopying, recording, or other electronic or mechanical methods, without the prior written permission of the publisher, except in the case of brief quotations embodied in critical reviews and certain other noncommercial uses permitted by copyright law.

References to historical events, real people, or real places are often fictitious. In such cases, the names, characters, and places are products of the author's imagination. We do this where it's important to protect the privacy of people, places, and things.

689 Burke Rd
Camberwell Victoria 3124
Australia

www.LearnWellBooks.com

We're led by God. Our business is also committed to supporting kids' charities. At the time of printing, we have donated well over $100,000 to enable mentoring services for underprivileged children. By choosing our books, you are helping children who desperately need it. Thank you.

**This is really important.
It's a sincere thank you.**

My name is Wayne, the founder of LearnWell.

My Dad put a book in my hands when I was 13. It was written by Zig Ziglar and it changed the course of my life. Since then, it's been books that have helped me get over breakups, learn how to be a good friend, study the lives of good people and books have been the source of my persistence through some pretty challenging times.

My purpose is now to return the favor. To create books that might be the turning point in the lives of people around the world, just like they've been for me. It's enough to almost bring me to tears to think of you holding this book, seeking information and wisdom from something that I've helped to create. I'm moved in a way that I can't fully explain.

We're a small and 'beyond-enthusiastic' team here at LearnWell. We're writers, editors, researchers, designers, formatters (oh ... and a bookkeeper!) who take your decision to learn with us incredibly seriously. We consider it a privilege to be part of your learning journey. Thank you for allowing us to join you.

If there's anything we did really well, anything we messed up, or anything AT ALL that we could do better, would you please write to us and tell us (like, right now!) We would love to hear from you!

readers@learnwellbooks.com

We're sending you our thanks, our love and our very best wishes.

Wayne
and the team at LearnWell Books.

WELCOME TO OUR COMMUNITY

"It's like a private online book club"

Imagine if you could actually meet and talk with other readers of this book and share your experiences.

Imagine if you could chat with the author or join them on a live Q&A!

Imagine getting access to the author's notes and other exclusive, unpublished material.

You can do all of that and a lot more in the LearnWell Online Community!!

→ Download your **Workbook**
→ Chat directly with the author!
→ Meet and feel supported by other readers and their experiences.
→ Access additional, exclusive content about this topic and others.
→ Join our live Author Q&A sessions online.
→ Learn faster, make lasting changes, and have 10 times more fun!

All of this is part of our commitment to creating the best learning resources in the world.

Scan the QR code to get FREE access
www.learnwellbooks.com/alive

CO-AUTHOR

Our internal team of writers creates our books. We collaborate together, research together, edit each other's manuscripts, and collectively take responsibility for the written work we produce.

Sometimes we will seek input from a subject matter expert who can add meaningful insight on a topic. We interview that expert, often adopt their tone and style and refer to them in the first person. On this occasion, we worked with ...

Dr. Deanna Rose

Deanna is a naturopathic doctor (ND), certified sports nutritionist (CISSN), strength and conditioning specialist (CSCS), and the founder of a client-centered health and wellness company rooted in functional and integrative nutrition and medicine, designed for high-performing people.

Deanna grew up as a competitive swimmer and has been a certified strength and conditioning specialist for over a decade. After going from constant burnout, chronic fatigue, and losing sight of her purpose, Deanna realized the importance of reconnecting physical, mental, and energetic human elements to prevent repeating destructive patterns and allow continuous growth to take place. She went from being exhausted all the time, having trouble losing weight, and having ridiculous mood swings to having the ability to summon energy on demand and realigning her mind and body performance.

Deanna is passionate about using her experience and expertise to help others reclaim their mental & physical health, optimize energy, and reconnect with their inner wisdom to achieve the personal success they desire.

To my parents
Your work ethic and resilience have
always and will continue to inspire me.

To Matt
Your unconditional love
and support is my light

CONTENTS

	Introduction	10
1	**The Burnout Ambulance**	16
	What Needs To Happen. Immediately.	
2	**Is This Really Burnout? Maybe I'm Just Tired?**	37
	The Three Stages Of Burnout And Why You Can't 'Just Get Over It'	
3	**Your Brilliant Future**	52
	How To Design Your Ideal Life … And Achieve It!	
4	**Your Path To Recovery**	59
	What To Focus On To Conquer Your Burnout	

PART 1: The Mind — 63

5	**Your Thoughts Can Heal You**	64
	The Surprising Ways Your Mindset Affects Your Physical Body	
6	**Change Your Mind, Change Your Life**	77
	Six Steps To Reprogram Your Limiting Beliefs For A More Fulfilling Life	
7	**Do Less, Get More**	90
	Five Steps To Replacing Your Bad Habits With Positive Ones	

PART 2: The Body   **101**

8 Puffy & Backed Up   102
The Shocking Impact Of Acute And Chronic Inflammation

9 Trust Your Gut   111
The Surprising Connection Between Gut Health And Burnout

10 Feed, Don't Deprive   124
How To Consume A Diet Which Genuinely Supports Your Health

11 The Domino Effect   131
Why A Holistic Approach Is The Only Way To Tackle Burnout

Conclusion   145

References   151

YOUR
WORKBOOK

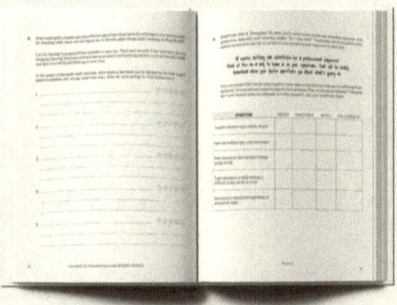

A shocking truth was discovered by a study done in 1987 – **people only remember 10% of what they read!**

That seems so discouraging.

But here's the **GOOD NEWS** – reading is **NEVER** a waste of time. As long as you do **one** important thing …

The same study (by National Training Laboratories) shows that you will remember 90% of what you read when you **put your new knowledge into action**!

Here at LearnWell, we aim to create **the world's best learning resources**. So, we have included a highly engaging **Workbook** that helps you put your new knowledge into fun, practical action.

So, make sure you download your **FREE Workbook.** You'll find it located inside the **LearnWell Community.** Simply scan the QR code below for access.

Get your Workbook in the LearnWell Community
Scan the QR Code for access or go to:
www.learnwellbooks.com/alive

INTRODUCTION

This is burnout. The sluggishness, the lack of interest, the skin problems, the fluctuating appetite. It's not just modern life. It's not just going to disappear. You're burnt out and the only way to regain yourself is to accept that this is not working. You're meant to feel better than this. And you can.

It doesn't help that we don't talk about burnout enough. And for those of us suffering from it, we hide it because we believe it will make people think we're weak or inadequate

But burnout is real and the numbers are frighteningly high. In 2021, Indeed.com reported that over 52% of the 1,500 people surveyed felt burnt out, up from 43% pre-pandemic.[1]

Looking at me now, people find it hard to believe that I went through a serious period of burnout when I was in med school. These days, I'm filled with energy and a zest for life. Back then, I had to nap 3-4 times a day just to make it through. I could just about stay on top of my work, but forget about any idea of fun. I simply wasn't capable of anything social, least of all parties or even hanging out with friends. I could only manage life's essential activities. And then only just.

This was no way to live.

But I was an overachiever. I'd always achieved my goals. I told myself I had to bootstrap my way out of it. *You got yourself into med school!* I told myself. *There's nothing you can't do!*

Introduction

I faced my burnout like I was studying for a major exam and I needed to get an A. I threw myself into finding the solution, ironically approaching it with the same attitude that had pushed me into burnout.

I tried everything - diets, workouts, supplements, meditations. If it was supposed to be a cure for burnout, I gave it a shot, but nothing lasted more than a few days. I was mentally and physically exhausted, my body totally depleted. Some days it was almost impossible to get out of bed in the morning. As if I wasn't feeling bad enough, failing to cure my burnout made me feel even worse.

I couldn't understand what had changed. I was a competitive swimmer in my youth. If you know anything about the sport, you'll understand that swimming at a high level involves early mornings, and hours of training. Then, after I'd been up since 5am and swam hundreds of lengths, I had to go to school and study all day - then I'd be back in the pool again after school was done. Next day, I did it all over again.

I was like a machine. In my late teens and early 20s, I could function on just 2 hours of sleep. Sleep was for wimps! I had too much to do to waste time lounging about in bed.

If you think that as a high performance athlete that I was treating my body like a temple, you'd be completely wrong. My diet was awful. I lived on processed food. If it was cheap and quick, I'd shovel it into my mouth. I didn't have time to cook. I was too busy training and studying.

In theory, given my lifestyle, I should have been shuffling around like a zombie. No one would ever recommend doing what I was doing to someone who wanted to enjoy a healthy lifestyle. But I was young and filled with energy. I had no problem doing whatever I wanted, day or night. Nothing was going to stand in my way. I felt like I was invincible.

That all changed when I was 27. I hit a wall and suddenly fell apart.

My mood was unpredictable. I never knew how I might feel in any situation. I was just as likely to laugh or cry. My period was all over the place. I had random breakouts on my face and body. I suffered constant headaches and random body aches. It was tough on me - and the people around me.

I lost all motivation. All those things that brought me joy couldn't get me excited anymore. Instead of only needing two hours' sleep, my bed became my new best friend. I needed twelve hours just to function at the bare minimum. I found myself needing to take regular naps throughout the day to top up my energy levels so I could meet essay deadlines. Even then, I constantly worried whether I'd be able to stay on top of my workload.

Happiness and my old quality of life were a dim and distant memory. I felt like I was a failure. All those things I used to take for granted were now an impossible dream. I told myself I was letting my loved ones down because I couldn't do all the things I used to do. My negative self-talk was overwhelming. I had a little voice in my mind that kept telling me I was useless.

I couldn't go on like that. I knew I wasn't useless. I was a woman with big dreams. I wasn't going to give up on them, so I went searching for answers.

Introduction

That journey of discovery led me to where I am today. Perpetual burnout and chronic fatigue are a thing of the past. Yes, I found the solution and it wasn't what I thought it would be.

These days, I don't have to worry about my energy levels. I'm overflowing with vigor. I'm back to doing whatever I want to do, whenever I want to do it. I get to enjoy life to its fullest, but these days I'm a lot more self-aware. I understand what causes burnout and what I need to do to make sure I never suffer from it again.

I'm grateful for my burnout. It's thanks to my experiences that I found my life's calling. My burnout is the reason I've chosen to focus on supporting high performing entrepreneurs who need a solution to their problems with minimal time and effort. I understand more than most the importance of long lasting solutions that don't involve taking hours out of your day to be mindful or meditate or disappearing off to a distant mountain so you can gaze at your navel in contemplative silence. While I'm not saying that these things can't be helpful or meaningful, they just don't suit everyone. Sometimes you just want to get rid of your burnout without having to radically overhaul your life.

But I know full well that it's not only entrepreneurs who struggle with burnout. It can hit anyone at any stage of their life, regardless of their circumstance. I want to help as many people as possible. *Nobody* should have to suffer from burnout. There is a solution - and it's in this book.

I've taken all the wisdom and insight I've gained from my own experiences and my work with others in this area and I've poured it into this easy to follow guide. Whether you're a solopreneur, high-flying executive, student, working parent, stay-at-home parent, caregiver, etc. you'll find the answers you've been looking for right here in these pages.

In the following chapters, you'll discover everything you need to know to banish burnout for good. You'll learn how to identify which stage of burnout you're currently suffering and why all those things you've been trying haven't worked. I'll give you a plan of attack for you to tailor to your specific needs. No two people are the same. No two people suffer burnout in the same way. Your plan needs to be designed to support your precise needs. You'll get the guidance you need to do just that.

One thing to note. While the program I'll share with you can be completed in as little as 30 days, please don't feel this is a hard and fast rule. Take whatever time you need. Work at your own pace. Sometimes, the thought of having to do something for 30 days can be overwhelming. So don't think about it! Simply do the exercises as you go along. Take each day as it comes and don't worry about what you're going to do tomorrow. Focus on today and how you can make it better than yesterday.

I know that when you start seeing results (and you will!) you'll be motivated to keep going with the program. When you've finished working through the exercises, you may even feel like you want to keep them up for the rest of your life. They'll be something you look forward to doing because you love how good they make you feel.

You're also going to need support as you recover. It would mean the world to me to see you and other readers leaning on each other in the LearnWell Community.

Introduction

But let's not get ahead of ourselves. For now, let's just take the first step. If you're ready to discover the permanent solution to your burnout, turn the page and let's get started.

Here's to the best possible version of you!

Dr. Deanna Rose
x

Guys, before moving on, grab the Workbook. It's an essential part of what I have to teach you.

1

THE BURNOUT AMBULANCE

What Needs To Happen.
Immediately.

It takes ten times as long to put yourself back together as it does to fall apart.

– Suzanne Collins

It's said that there are several stages to acceptance. The final one being acceptance itself. Whatever it is you need to accept, you'll likely deny it first, then become angry about it and try to bargain your way out of it but eventually you'll have to accept the facts in front of you.

Your facts are indisputable - you're burnt out. There may still be stubborn elements of non-acceptance lingering but seeing as you've chosen to read this particular book, I'd say the case can now be closed.

People don't readily accept their burnout. That's one of the principal causes of burnout - the persistent, belligerent denial that anything's wrong. It may have taken you months, if not, years to arrive at the point where you're finally prepared to accept that this approach to your life is killing you.

However long it's taken to get here, you're now finally ready to do something about it. Although, something that took you this long to develop and ultimately accept won't disappear in the time that your impatience would like it to. Your recovery time is its very own source of therapy. If the solution was simple or quick, you'd take it. Then, knowing that it was readily available, you'd enter a cycle of burnout and recovery that would see no end.

That it takes some time to undo means that you'll be far less likely to adopt the same destructive approach again in the future. The sustained solution to your burnout includes new thinking, new practices and a mindset that will not just help you recover but, in fact, change. You will emerge from this process altogether stronger, wiser and far more capable. You'll affect everyone around you with a healthy, calm resilience instead of a state of panic and haste. You'll smile more, laugh more and solve problems with the clarity and precision of a razor instead of bashing every problem with a sledgehammer.

Your solution is here and it's ready but you may not be ... yet. You're cooked. Your heart rate is high for prolonged periods and it's uncorrelated to your level of physical activity. At a glance, your skin may indicate your ill-health. Your nervous system bristles like the hairs on a cat's back. Your digestive system is overwhelmed and dysfunctional. You're the equivalent of a car crash victim. You don't need physio or rehab. That can wait. You need urgent treatment to stabilize your condition so that you can be safely transported to the 'burnout recovery ward' for the proper care you need.

This first chapter is your burnout ambulance. The first responders on the scene of your incident. It's the collection of activities you need to undertake right now to create physical and mental stability in your life.

Once that's established, then I'll guide you through the process that I've built for your sustained recovery. But right now, we need to get your heart rate back down, your mind clear and to restore some degree of control over your time.

But be warned. You will do these things because they're straightforward and relatively easy. Then you'll think that you're done. You're fixed!

You're not.

Don't stop at the first sign of recovery. Follow me through. I've been down this path myself and I've taken hundreds of people down the same path. It's a journey of discovery and of valuable life change. Both for you and for the people you care about and who are most likely very worried about you right now. They need you to do this as much as you need to do this.

This is triage. This is not the recovery ward. Start here. Do these things. They work. You need them. They will give you the strength to do the transformative work that's to come.

STOP!

Seriously. Just stop. You have to.

"But I can't!"

You can.

"But the whole world will collapse!"

It won't

"But who will do the things?"

Someone. Or no one. Just not you. For now.

Stop. Now. This is non-negotiable.

Your self-identity could probably be described as 'high achiever'. Whatever profession, hobby or activity you've chosen to burn yourself out on, you're not the person taking extra breaks, shirking your responsibilities or setting clear boundaries around your time. You're the first there and the last to leave and, as for time off, you probably don't acknowledge the importance or even the validity of it. You probably think that rest is unproductive.

For now, you need to do less. You need to create time for rest in your routine, as a matter of extreme urgency. You know what urgency means, right? Just make rest as urgent as everything else you think is urgent. Ironically, this will make you more productive, not less. When you allow yourself to rest, you replenish your energy. You allow your brain to stop burning so much energy. Did you realize that, despite only representing 2% of your overall weight, your brain burns 20% of your body's energy. You can't think, learn or assimilate new information without consuming huge amounts of energy and you can't do any of that when you've got no energy.

Similarly, when you exercise, rest days are an important part of your program. Without them, you end up damaging your body, not improving your fitness. So it is with your brain. Giving yourself one day off a week (preferably two) allows your brain to recover and to operate at optimum capacity when you do return to peak mental activity.

Make time to rest. Now. Whether it's a 2-week holiday or an afternoon off, stop what you're doing and rest. You don't need to disappear into the forest or hop on the next plane out of town. In fact, the less travel, the better.

Create as much time as you can possibly find for yourself. Your first level is to simply rest. Sleep. Walk slowly. Read for fun and enjoyment. Your next level is self-care. A spa day. A massage. A luxurious lunch. Anything relaxing.

I know there will be resistance. When you've been the one to take on everyone's tasks and problems, they will not react well when you stop doing that. In fact, people will present all sorts of challenges to your attempt to regain control of your own time and health. You may need to go to extraordinary lengths to achieve this essential break. You may need doctor's certificates. You may need to become familiar with your employer's mental health policy. You may have to trust people with responsibilities that they're not used to.

Whatever you have to do, do it. It is highly unlikely that anything that is preventing you from taking this break is as important as the break itself. Tell them it's not permanent. You are coming back. However, you may also like to tell them that when you do come back, things are going to be changing around here. Starting with ...

SET BOUNDARIES

'No' is a complete sentence. It is one of the most important words in your vocabulary. Get comfortable with saying it, because you may have to use it a lot while you establish your new way of doing things.

If this is a new thing for you, try practicing it in low-risk situations so you can build confidence in saying no. Say no to members of your team before saying no to your boss. Say no to your kids before you say no to your spouse. Say no to your friends. Say no to the street vendors who try to sell you things you don't need. Say no to the things that aren't good for you. Say no to the things you don't want. The more you say it and discover that nothing bad happens as a consequence, the easier it will be for you to say it in situations where it really matters.

Another simple trick is to insert a thoughtful pause before you say 'yes' to anything. Next time someone asks you to take on another task that they are equally capable of doing, take a moment to think. Check-in with yourself to see if you're *really* comfortable with doing what you've been asked to do. If you need some time to figure out how to say no, you could buy yourself some time by saying, "That could work. Let me check what I've got on and I'll get back to you."

During your rest time that you've recently organized (!), decide where your boundaries are going to lie. Make a list of all the things you feel you're being held accountable for. Where there is another party responsible for the things you're accountable for, like a boss, children or a spouse, ask them to do the same thing so you can discuss them after your rest period. Chances are high that you'll have very different ideas about what you should be doing.

If you're a full time parent, make a list based on your role in the home and compare notes with your partner to see if you both have realistic expectations.

When you return from your rest, sit down with your boss, kids, partner or otherwise and between you, prioritize what you need to do and what you can let go of. It may even be that you've been doing things you don't need to do and have taken on extra roles unnecessarily.

As you agree on your responsibilities, remember to use your 'no' to set realistic expectations.

If you're discussing your duties with your boss, you should also look into other ways your employers can help you live more healthily. Maybe flexitime is an option or you could job share. Perhaps there is some software or equipment that could help you work more efficiently and alleviate some of the mental burden of your work.

More recently, working remotely has become a more accepted option. Many have discovered that they don't need to spend as much time in the office or don't even need to go in at all. Look at the lessons learned by others as far as the workplace is concerned and see whether you can apply them to your situation. That stressful commute might not be essential. You could have more time with your family if you're not spending an hour or more on the road every day.

You can also do what's called a 'boundary audit.' This is where you pay attention to what people and situations stress you out. Record in your Workbook whenever you notice something. These will be areas where you'll need to establish or reinforce a boundary.

Think about where you need to set limits in your life. Maybe you're not going to check work emails beyond 7pm at night. Perhaps you won't answer the phone when you're not on call. You could get a second phone you use solely for work (if you don't already) so you know you can switch it off and leave it off when it's outside office hours.

It's no good setting boundaries if no one else knows what they are. Communicate them to the people around you so there's no misunderstanding. If they can't contact you after a certain time, let them know exactly when you will take calls or check emails. If you

CONQUER

don't want to hear from work while you're on vacation unless it's an emergency, tell them exactly what an emergency means to you.

When a boundary is broken (and it's bound to happen at some point), deal with it immediately. It's much better to reinforce your new way of being when it happens than letting it slide. Otherwise, people will think they can ignore them and you'll soon slip back into old habits and routines.

BRAIN DUMP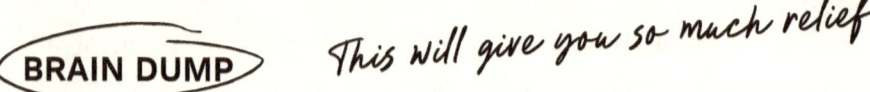

One of the most harrowing feelings that burnout delivers is the constant, churning loop of thoughts that are impossible to escape. You could be having dinner with your family, watching your kids play basketball, trying to read or, worse, trying to sleep and the noise from your mind is loud and relentless. The quieter you are, the louder it becomes. The more you try to relax, the more it demands your energy and attention.

The constant roar of tasks, problems, people, appointments and ideas keeps you from being present and, ironically, keeps you from having the clarity required to handle any of these things well.

You need to get all of this out, onto paper. It all needs to exit your head. Take a pen and several pages and start writing. Pour it all out. The meeting times, the ideas, the sketches, list of things to do, the plans you're making, the problems you're having, the people you need to call, the people whose calls you've missed ... write it all down. Don't stop until the noise stops.

Throughout your process with me, keep doing this. Any time the noise in your head gets loud and you're finding it hard to concentrate or to be present, it's time to write.

I've created a Workbook for you that I'll refer to often throughout this book. You can't just read about the solution to burnout. That will never work. You're too preoccupied to pay enough attention to words sitting idly on a page. You've got to take action to solve a problem like this. After all, it's your actions that created the problem. Just reading isn't enough to overcome that.

Your Workbook includes a collection of powerful exercises for you to do. Those activities will deliver your long-term solution to burnout. At the very back of the Workbook you'll notice I've included a collection of pages that are for your Brain Dump. Go there now and do that. It will provide enormous relief.

Get your free copy of the Workbook at www.learnwellbooks.com/alive

PUT SYSTEMS IN PLACE

When you're establishing the new habits you'll learn about in this book, it's a good idea to put systems in place that support them.

For example, Tim Ferris, author of *The 4-Hour Workweek* says,

"Never automate something that can be eliminated, and never delegate something that can be automated or streamlined."

He was writing for entrepreneurs, but this is just as true if you're working for someone else or you're a full time parent or carer. This principle also applies to charity work, domestic duties or anything else that's got you frazzled. You might decide you're going to delegate cleaning to a professional or automate meals by signing up to a meal prep subscription, for example.

There are four steps to this process:

- Eliminate
- Automate
- Delegate
- Procrastinate

Firstly, look at your to-do list and think about whether each task really needs to be done. Do you enjoy doing it? (If you don't enjoy most of the tasks you have to do at work, now might be the time to find a new job you *do* enjoy...) Is it essential? Is it generating revenue or an important outcome for the business? Will the world end if you don't do it? If you're brutally honest with yourself, you'll probably find many jobs that simply don't need to be done.

For example, you might be posting a lot on social media, but when you do this exercise, you realize your clients find you more frequently through word of mouth or search engines. You can cross social media off your list.

If you're finding it hard to eliminate tasks that aren't producing results, remind yourself that life's too short to hate your job. If a task doesn't have any value, it's out of here!

Now you're left with a list of tasks that need to be done one way or another. If there are repetitive tasks or processes on that list, consider whether you can automate them. You may need to invest in some apps, but you'll save so much time (and money) in the long run.

You might like to start with a calendar scheduling software to organize your time. If you're still posting on social media, look into automation tools to schedule your posts so you spend less time on them.

Now you've eliminated or automated as much as possible, now think about whether you can delegate it. Are you *really* the best person for each job? If you're not a qualified designer, it's worth bringing one in. You might think your copy is great, but an experienced writer can probably generate a lot more leads for you.

Think about the people around you - you probably know people who can take over jobs that are far better suited to their skills than yours. If you're doing this exercise to make your home life easier, think about what tasks you could give to other family members. Teenagers are more than capable of doing their own laundry and cleaning up after themselves. You and your partner could take it in turns to cook dinner. It's easy to believe that if you don't do it either it won't get done or it won't get done to your standards. Is that really true?

Sure, your teen might not be as diligent at scrubbing the bathroom, but how are they going to get better if they're not allowed to practice? A toddler might not be amazing at tidying up after themselves, but if you get them in the habit from an early age, it's much easier to keep them involved in the housework when they're older.

Finally, you get to procrastinate - yes. But this is helpful procrastination. In this case, you deliberately put off a task so you can get other, more important, things done first. Like resting. Procrastination is likely an unflexed muscle of yours. You don't put anything off. You do everything without discernment. You don't carefully decide whether it warrants your time or even observe what the consequences are if you don't do it. You're just programmed to do everything. Try not doing things. Put them off. See what happens. See who else does them. See if they even matter. Many won't and you'll have effectively eliminated them from your future schedule.

BRACE FOR PUSHBACK

Just because you've decided to do things differently doesn't mean everyone else is going to be on board. While you're establishing your new boundaries, you're going to experience negative reactions from others. This is a good thing, even though it may not feel like it at the time. It shows you were right to put that boundary in place and it's doing its job.

You may find it helpful to imagine scenarios when your boundaries are pushed and consider what you'll do when it happens. That way, when you inevitably face the situation in real life, you'll be better equipped to deal with it in a calm, logical fashion rather than giving a knee jerk, emotional reaction.

ADJUST YOUR WORK-LIFE BALANCE

You hear talk of a healthy work-life balance a lot, but how many of us actually manage to achieve it? Let your burnout be your wake up call that you need to be one of the ones who do.

The first thing I told you to do in this chapter was to rest. It's so important I'm going to remind you to do it again. This includes regular breaks throughout your normal days. Even microbreaks for a cup of tea, or a walk around the office to stretch your legs. This will:

- Improve concentration
- Lower stress
- Keep you engaged in a task
- Make work more fun[3]

Since our brains naturally become fatigued after 90 minutes of performing a task[4], make a commitment to yourself to take 15 minutes' down time every hour and a half or so. This lets your brain reset and get back to the task with renewed vigor.

Take your lunch break. Do not work while you eat at your desk. Take. A. Break.

Try to eat mindfully. This is when you slow right down and focus on every little aspect of the process. Before you place your food in your mouth, visually examine it with child-like curiosity. Notice its appearance and texture. Smell it. Close your eyes and really observe the aroma.

Only then should you put your food in your mouth. Chew slowly and deliberately, noticing how the texture of the food changes as you do. Savor the taste and only swallow when you're ready. You might like to take a moment to feel grateful for the food and really appreciate the moment.

Eating mindfully will help you enjoy your food more. It will support new healthy eating habits (which we will cover in a later chapter) and help your digestive system.[5]

Be kind to yourself. You are not superhuman! Acknowledge and work within your limits instead of thinking you can do it all. You've already learned you can't - the hard way. Release the need for control and your sense of perfectionism. Trying to live up to an impossible standard will only cause your burnout to rebound with added permanence.

Life isn't always easy. Even someone who makes it look effortless will be struggling behind the scenes. You're going to make mistakes and that's okay. Recognize that life is a series of learning opportunities that enable you to grow instead of beating yourself up for any mistakes. This will help you feel more balanced in life overall.

YOUR WORK-LIFE BALANCE AT HOME

It's just as important to change how you do things at home as it is at work if you're going to find the right balance of priorities. Make sure everyone knows when your office hours are over so you can genuinely unplug when you're at home. Set up an autoresponder in your emails so if anyone tries to contact you when you're unavailable they know when to expect a reply. This will also help you be disciplined and not check your work email - you'll have the reassurance of knowing they're already being dealt with.

Nurture the relationships that are important to you. You've likely been neglecting your relationships because you had your priorities confused. Humans are social creatures and even introverts need human contact for optimal mental health.

If you've been too focused on work, it's time to start reconnecting with friends and family. Since you're no longer available for work after a certain time, you've now got an opportunity to spend time with the people you love.

Make time in your schedule for friends and family. This is as non-negotiable as any important business meeting. Talk to the people you want to be with and make sure the time you're setting aside works for all of you - you'll all need to put in the effort to heal your relationships. You might also like to call or video chat with people who live further away. It may be that some relationships have deteriorated past the point of repair. Let this be a reminder to you of how important it is to nurture those you value. Maybe you'll be able to rebuild those friendships when you're further along your healing journey.

It's also possible that you realize that some relationships aren't good for you. Don't be afraid to let go of toxic people in your life who will try to pull you back to your old ways.

Consider the things and people which truly bring you joy. Maybe you like doing jigsaw puzzles or going to the movies. Perhaps you used to love dancing or swimming but haven't done it for years.

Now's the time to get back to those old activities you've let slide - or discover new interests by doing something you've always wanted to do but never got round to it. Make sure you include spending quality time by yourself so you can re-energize and keep your focus on the things that matter to you.

FIND AN ACCOUNTABILITY PARTNER

It's easy to become isolated as an adult. Self-care falls way down our list of priorities as we become consumed by work and the pressures of adulting. While this burnout triage may seem straightforward, you're looking at undoing unhealthy habits you've held for a long time. Burnout has become your comfort zone, even though it's a very uncomfortable place to be. Without someone to help you stay on track, you may unwittingly slide back into old ways of doing things.

An accountability partner is someone you can check in with on a regular basis to discuss your progress. They'll cheer you on and help you practice kindness towards yourself. If you struggle with any aspect of the program, they can talk you through ways to get you back on track.

The way you're feeling right now, you'll probably find it difficult to muster the energy to do the daily work you need to get over your burnout. Checking in with your accountability partner every day will make it easier for you to take a few minutes every day to look up the next step in the process and incorporate it into your routine.

Your accountability partner could be:

- A friend
- Family
- A colleague
- Someone from your church
- A mentor

Anyone you know that will provide unconditional, non-judgmental support as you recover from your burnout can be an accountability partner. When you have one, you won't feel so alone and you'll have someone who can help you through the tough times, just as you'll support them in turn.

Remember that an accountability partner will only be helpful if you use them. If this is something you struggle with, use your Workbook to consider:

- When am I willing to ask for help?
- When have I asked for help in the past? What happened?
- How do I feel when I ask for help? What do I think will happen?
- Do I have negative or positive expectations surrounding asking for help?

Identify one problem you would like help with right now. Find one person you can ask for help, then ask them!

STRESS MANAGEMENT TECHNIQUES

In this book, you'll be provided a number of stress management methods which you should incorporate into your daily life. Simple activities you might like to try before diving into the program include:

Meditation. The simplest form of meditation is to focus on your breath. It's as simple as it sounds - close your eyes and concentrate on the flow of your breath in and out of your body. However, for many overachieving types, this can be too passive, so you might like to try something more active, such as chanting a mantra silently in your mind. You could use a mantra that supports the positive mindset you want to develop, such as *I am calm, I am worthy,* or *I am happy*. Sit comfortably with your back supported, close your eyes and repeat your chosen mantra over and over. Start with a few minutes a day (two is plenty) and gradually extend the amount of time you meditate until you can comfortably do twenty minutes or more. It's best to build up slowly like this so you have a positive experience with meditation and feel like you can do it and it's easy. If you overcommit yourself and try to do too long, you'll find it hard to maintain your focus. This will make you disheartened and lose the motivation to stick with your meditation practice.

Yoga. Just as with meditation, there are many different styles from the passive forms of Hatha yoga to the more dynamic Ashtanga. See what classes are available and try out a few to discover which one you like most.

Coloring. Adult coloring books are increasingly popular. Look for ones with complex abstract designs like mandalas or plaid so you can lose yourself in the image and let go of the distractions of your surroundings.

Drumming. Meeting up with a group of people and pounding out some beats is fun and helps ease you into being in the moment.

Morning pages. Simply write out your stream of consciousness first thing in the morning. Whatever's on your mind. If you can't think of anything, write that! I can't think of anything or reflect on how you're feeling this morning. How did you feel when your alarm went off? How did it feel when your feet first touched the ground this morning? How did that first sip of coffee taste when it touched your lips? These morning pages are simply an opportunity for you to reflect on your experiences and bring them to your consciousness.

Walking. Get yourself out in the fresh air and go for a good walk. Bonus points if you can walk in a natural environment.

The impact of these activities is subtle and progressive. But you *will* notice a negative impact immediately if you stop! Even though it's a gradual, positive benefit, make relaxation and stress management a part of your daily routine starting today. It will make a huge difference to your life.

THERAPY AND COUNSELING

Throughout this book, I'm going to empower you with practices you can do yourself without the need of external support, but sometimes we're simply too close to a situation to be able to figure it out on our own. This is why I've recommended an accountability partner. However, you may not have someone who can take on this role for you or you may feel you need extra support right now.

There is no shame in asking for help. Speaking to a trained professional can help you gain clarity and support you as you navigate this new way of doing things. It takes a lot of courage, energy, and willpower to establish different habits. Getting help from a therapist will help you show kindness and compassion to yourself as you adjust to your new lifestyle. They can show you a different perspective and let you know that one hiccup doesn't mean you have to abandon this new approach and it doesn't undermine all your hard work.

Throughout this whole process, I'll regularly emphasize the importance of you and the decisions you make for yourself. This is the right time to put yourself first and it will help to find someone who will remind you to do so because, if we're honest, you haven't done a great job of that on your own.

You've now been given a few things to get temporary relief from your burnout and you can build on that. In the rest of this book, we're going to cover a comprehensive program designed to give you permanent results.

If you think you're feeling a little better right now, you're going to feel amazing by the time you're done with this book! Read on to take your first permanent steps on the road to recovery.

2

IS THIS REALLY BURNOUT? MAYBE I'M JUST TIRED?

The Three Stages Of Burnout And Why You Can't 'Just Get Over It'

The land of burnout is not a place I ever want to go back to.

– Arianna Huffington

"I don't know where to start."

The woman sitting in my office was perched on the edge of the chair, nervously wringing her hands. She didn't seem to be able to stay still. She was constantly fidgeting, playing with her hair, fiddling with the buttons on her top. Well dressed and well spoken, she wouldn't have looked out of place in a high powered board meeting, but right now, she seemed on the verge of tears.

"It's okay." I smiled to reassure her. "Why don't you try telling me a little about what brought you here?"

"I am - I *was* - a manager at a big consulting firm. I worked for them for fifteen years and I used to love it. I thrived on working in a team filled with intelligent, motivated people and it was such a buzz working with other businesses to help them achieve their goals.

"I was mainly involved in the pitching and onboarding side of the business, which was pretty intense. I was good at what I did. We won most of our contracts, so then we'd have to go through an even more intense period of interviewing, researching, presenting to panels before passing our recommendations on to the relevant department. Unfortunately, sometimes our findings would show the need for redundancies, so many people resented our help."

"That must have been hard." I knew how she felt. I'd been in many high-pressure work situations myself and I remembered feeling like I always had to be 'on', I always had to perform.

"It was." She nodded. "I remember the first time I started losing confidence in my abilities. I was preparing to do some interviews for a new contract and I went way overboard preparing. I'd never felt so nervous, but this time I doubted everything I was doing. I had that tense, nervous feeling in my stomach, you know, when you feel constantly on edge?"

"Oh yeah." I nodded sympathetically.

"Maybe it was nerves or maybe it was adrenaline. I don't know. I just knew I wasn't feeling right, yet no one else seemed to notice something was wrong. And I was still meeting all my targets and then some. I was still getting a massive buzz from work, but I was feeling like I had to do more and more just to stay where I was.

"Not long after that, I was promoted. I had more responsibility and was in charge of a number of teams in different regions, but I was still really hands-on with new pitches. I desperately needed some help, but although I asked for it, I kept being told I was doing a great job, I didn't need anyone else and besides, there wasn't the budget."

"And meanwhile you were sinking deeper and deeper underwater?"

"That's right." She sighed. "I was becoming more isolated too. I was given my own office, but it was in a different building, so I was away from my old team. Besides, many of them had left because they found it too stressful. I had to do so much traveling, I had no time to build closer ties with my new colleagues.

"I started falling behind. I'd arrange meetings with my manager, but couldn't find the time to write out my notes so I'd forget to tell her important points. She seemed to think I was doing fine. Whenever I asked her for more support, she'd say I didn't need it.

I guess it was because I was still coming up with innovations and always seemed so in control. I was presenting a positive front to the world, but it was because I was terrified that if people saw the truth, they'd think I was a failure."

"OK. What happened next?"

"I started going further and further downhill. I was struggling to concentrate for long periods and I didn't have the energy to ferret out all the details of the new companies we were working with. I was running out of mental and physical energy and couldn't replenish it. Yet all I could think about was how I'd had this promotion and I didn't want to let anyone down. I felt like I'd be a failure if I let people see how much I was struggling, so I lied if anyone asked how I was doing and said I was fine. Instead, I was feeling on the verge of tears all the time, weak and tense, like I'd just thrown-up.

"There were times I'd close the door to my office and sit with my head in my hands, unable to face the thought of doing any work. At the same time, I felt like I was handling the stress just fine. Pretty stupid, huh?"

"It's not stupid at all," I said. "Lots of people go through the same thing when they're burnt out. What other symptoms did you have?"

"I was getting hot flushes, I couldn't focus for long and I was tired all the time. It didn't help that I was going through menopause, so I figured it was all because of that. But although my doctor put me on HRT, it didn't help and it got to the point where I was constantly fatigued. I'd sleep for ten hours straight and wake up exhausted. When I got home, I often didn't even have the energy to make dinner. On weekends I'd be working instead of resting. I felt like I had to work all the time or I'd fall behind. I was putting more and more pressure on myself to perform, but I'd lost all interest in my work. I was going through the motions because I had to, not because I wanted to."

"OK. Keep going."

"Then I got lucky, if you can call it that. I went back to the doctor to discuss my menopause symptoms, but my regular doctor wasn't available, so I had to see a locum. When I told her what had been happening, she started asking me questions and it all came tumbling out. She signed me off work for 3 months due to stress and exhaustion. I knew I'd been feeling bad, but it was weird to have a doctor tell me that there was something officially, medically wrong. For that first month, I did nothing but sleep. I was genuinely burnt out.

"Work kept calling me to ask what to do with the contracts I was responsible for. I couldn't escape even though I'd been signed off. So I handed in my notice. They begged me to stay, offered to get the help I'd been asking for, even said they'd restructure things and create a brand new position for me. I could pick and choose the contracts I worked on. It was too little too late. I felt like my job had stripped me of everything. I was a shadow of my former self."

She looked me straight in the eye. "So that's what's brought me here. I know some of the people you've worked with. Can you help me like you helped them?"

I smiled. "Yes. I can."

Amy (not her real name) is just one of my clients, but her story is very familiar. So many people come to me because they've hit a wall they didn't realize they were heading for until it was too late.

Burnout is tricky to identify. You may have picked up this book because you're so run down you can't work anymore. But burnout doesn't always look like this. You can work while you're burned out, but feel like every day is a bad day. You may lack motivation to get started on your work or feel depressed at the thought of doing anything. You might feel overwhelmed by your responsibilities and look to distract yourself with unhelpful coping mechanisms like drinking or social media.

Your burnout symptoms will vary depending on what stage you're at. You may be experiencing sleep disturbances, irritability and mood swings if you're in the first stage. If your burnout has progressed to the second or third stage, you'll also be dealing with a drop in energy levels and lack of motivation.

My research and experience have led me to this conclusion:

BURNOUT AND ADRENAL FATIGUE

It's not the inevitable consequence of our burnout culture. It's not stress. Nor overwhelm. It's not your never ending to-do list nor your feelings of inadequacy. Of course, these things can build up and get you into a state of burnout, but plenty of people experience these things without becoming burnt out. It is my belief there's a physical cause behind your burnout. Once you understand this, you'll know why you feel this way when you haven't in the past.

You'll understand why you're burnt out whereas your friends and colleagues may not be.

And the good news is that since there's a physical cause, there's a cure. Deal with your adrenal fatigue and you'll deal with your burnout.

There are three stages of adrenal fatigue. Here's a breakdown of what to expect at each stage:

Stage 1: Entry Phase Adrenal Fatigue

At the first stage of burnout, you'll have been dealing with stress for a while. Now you're starting to feel the impact of it on your body, energy, and performance. You may even have thought "If this keeps up, I might not make it." You might have noticed some weight gain. Brain fog has descended and you can't stop your mind racing. You're exhausted all the time, but you can't get to sleep because you're preoccupied.

Entry phase adrenal fatigue is the start of a slippery slope if you don't deal with it effectively. Your body is currently in overdrive, needing way more energy and resources than usual. If you don't counter this, your body can go into a state of depletion. You'll start experiencing other unwanted long-term symptoms and conditions.

Stage 2 - Mid Phase Adrenal Fatigue

If you're at stage 2, you'll be experiencing more intense symptoms originating from a few different organ systems. Maybe you've been feeling under the weather, moodier, or you lack motivation. Rather than feeling invigorated after a workout, you'll have lower energy. You'll wake up feeling exhausted. You may even ask yourself, "What's the point?"

Your body has been depleted for quite a while now as it deals with all these external and internal demands. If your stress response isn't properly dealt with, your body will continue to use up energy and resources as it tries to bring all systems back to equilibrium.

You may be struggling with weight gain or finding it hard to lose fat. You may be dealing with constant brain fog and a poor memory. You're exhausted when you wake up and throughout the day. You may have a low libido. You may feel there's never enough time to get everything done.

Mid phase adrenal fatigue is characterized by overwhelm, exhaustion and the frequent urge to nap. You'll have lost interest in those things which used to excite you. Even those espressos you used to throw back no longer work.

Stage 3 - Late Phase Adrenal Fatigue

It's been a while. A long while. You've thought about giving up. You've asked, "What's the point?" You've tried all the tricks and hacks you found online, but nothing's worked.

By now you could be experiencing a range of symptoms, from low mood to irritability, absolute exhaustion, brain fog, anxiety attacks, the constant need to nap, no libido or a failing memory. You may find it impossible to recall a time when you didn't feel this way. If you're female, you may also be suffering irregular menstrual cycles. Your periods may have stopped completely.

Your body has been depleted for so long it's no longer able to return itself to a state of balance. The symptoms you're experiencing are a full reflection of an inability to return to a state of homeostasis. During this phase, your body's ability to carry out basic functions is severely reduced. Old symptoms increase in intensity. To add insult to injury, new symptoms come up.

Late phase adrenal fatigue is filled with exhaustion, helplessness, missed work, and even existential crises. You have no interest in anything, not even the things you used to love the most. Nothing seems to go in your favor. You question whether you'll ever have energy or feel happy again.

It's no surprise to hear that, whatever stage of burnout you're at, it will impact on all areas of your life. For most people, the most common sign of burnout is when their stress levels are so high they become less and less effective at work. You lose all interest in work or life. Relationships suffer because you lack the motivation to devote time, energy, and attention to them. The career which was once so important to you seems unfulfilling and pointless.

As for that drive and ambition which has taken you so far? Forget about it. What's even worse is you *know* you're capable of more, but you just don't seem to be able to achieve your regular output. And so you're stuck in a downward spiral, where the less you do, the more you beat yourself up, and you're able to do even less.

Unfortunately, unlike depression, there's no such thing as an official diagnosis of burnout or adrenal fatigue. So you may struggle to get support because it gets dismissed as 'just' stress. Sometimes the terms 'burnout' or 'adrenal fatigue' can be used as a catch-all description for a collection of symptoms such as fatigue, body aches, nervousness, sleep disturbances, and digestive problems. Burnout can also start to look more like depression. Burnout is insidious. It creeps up on you when you're least expecting it. You may be experiencing all the symptoms yet still not realize that's what's going on.

Burnout can hit anyone. It's important to understand that burnout doesn't only occur because you've got too much on your plate. It can also happen if your mindset changes. You may have been coping with an intense workload for years without any issues. It's only recently you've started feeling worn out. You might start resenting the demands placed on you by your job. You might wonder why you suddenly can't handle your job. And it might not be because your job is taking too much from you. It might simply be that you started feeling unappreciated and ignored and it's this shift in attitude which has started you on the path to burnout.

SELF-CARE ISN'T SELFISH

You've probably heard that it's important to look after yourself first before you consider anyone else. You may even feel bad that you've been neglecting yourself and allowed things to get so bad. As a consequence, you may have done some research for yourself on what you could do to heal your burnout. If so, you probably came across suggestions like these:

- Improving or cleaning your diet
- Get more exercise
- Wake up earlier
- Meditation or breathwork

Is This Really Burnout? Maybe I'm Just Tired?

- Go out with your friends more
- Follow stress management strategies that work for others
- Do more self-care activities such as going to the spa, having a massage, taking a day off to go somewhere nice, etc.

All great advice, right? But it doesn't work!

Why? Well, there's a number of reasons. It could be that you're only making surface level changes which aren't digging deep into the root cause. So it's pointless changing what you eat when the problem is your stress hormones. Working out more isn't going to help if you need to chill out and rest.

It might be that what you're trying is a one-off practice which isn't going to effect long-term change. One massage isn't going to ease away burnout which has built up after a year of overworking.

It could be that you're trying out random strategies which could potentially work but you're not giving them enough time to have an effect. Changing your diet might help, but if you're expecting it to transform your life after just a couple of weeks, you're going to be disappointed. So when nothing changes, you go back to your old diet because all that processed, high-sugar-and-fat foods is so comforting.

WHY ME?

It's perfectly normal to ask why you're the one suffering like this. It's so unfair! The reality is, burnout doesn't discriminate. It can affect you regardless of background, circumstance, or career. You can be a stay at home parent and suffer with burnout as much as a chief executive. Students can develop it while studying, caregivers can get burnt out from hours of looking after other people, people working in a service-based position might become burnt out after constantly having to consider other peoples' needs.

Regardless of your position, one common thread does seem to appear in most people with burnout - high achieving perfectionists. There are a number of potential reasons for this. Many of us are driven by feeling unworthy or not good enough. We push ourselves to achieve great things because we've got a deep-seated need to prove ourselves. Yet no matter how much we do, how many accolades we get, we still don't feel good enough.

High-achievers frequently have a need to be in control of their surroundings. We kid ourselves that we need to work more to achieve more so we can finally have the control we crave.

This can all be founded in a strong desire to gain approval from an authority figure we had in childhood or early adulthood - even if they're no longer around.

It's a lot to consider, isn't it?

If this resonates with you, take heart. I'm going to walk you through the process of recovery from burnout so you never have to worry about it again.

WHERE ARE YOU NOW?

Before we start digging into how you can relegate burnout to a distant memory, we need to take stock of where you are. There's no judgment attached to this process. It's important to know how far you are into burnout so you can be realistic about your recovery time. In my work, I've found that a lot of people are dismissive of how bad it really is. Then, because they think it's not that bad, they get frustrated because they don't experience an overnight cure.

I want you to experience permanent relief from burnout. That won't happen if you have unrealistic expectations of how this process will work. It's a step-by-step journey where each step forward builds on the previous one.

In addition, once you identify those symptoms which are your burnout speaking and not simply a normal state of being, you'll be able to see when you're making progress. Self-awareness makes it much easier for you to realize that things are changing for the better. As you see your symptoms melting away, you'll be motivated to keep going because you know the process works!

So, let's take inventory of your current burnout symptoms.

CHECK ALL THAT APPLY

How many of these symptoms are you experiencing? There is space in your Workbook to record the ones you have encountered.

- Bloating
- Gas
- Stomach Cramps
- Acid Reflux

- Loose stool
- Constipation
- Alternating between loose stool and constipation
- Irregular eating pattern
- Sugar cravings
- Brain fog
- Poor memory
- Poor sleep
- Fatigue
- Mood fluctuations
- Irritability
- Low mood
- Energy fluctuations throughout the day
- Weight fluctuations
- Unintentional weight gain / loss
- Muscle aches/ joint pain (no known injuries)
- Dry skin
- Breakouts on your face
- Irregular menstrual cycle
- Painful periods

OK. Now you've acknowledged your current state of burnout which is the first step on the road to recovery. But what will recovery look like? It may be so long since you felt 'normal' that you've forgotten what it's like. The thought of recovery may seem overwhelming at this point. Getting back to normal could even sound scary. How can you know who you are without your burnout?

I get it. There were times when I looked to the future and could see nothing but despair. That's why we're going to look at what you can expect when you've completed the healing process in the next chapter. I'll take you by the hand and lead you through what life can be like when your burnout is a thing of the past. I'll remind you why it is you picked up this book in the first place.

There *is* hope. There *is* life without burnout. Let's find out what that's going to look like.

 If you haven't already done so, please make sure you've become familiar with your Workbook. Go there before you move ahead. You'll draw a lot of value from the exercises that relate to Chapters 1 & 2.

YOUR BRILLIANT FUTURE

How To Design Your Ideal Life ... And Achieve It!

If you get tired, learn to rest - not to quit.

– Banksy

"When I was burned out and exhausted, all I could think about was surviving," Lynette confided in me. "Everything was about me but I had lost sight of who I was and who I wanted to be. Instead, all I could think about was what wasn't working, how exhausted I was all the time, how frustrated I was that I couldn't just bootstrap my way through how I was feeling."

"And now?" I prompted.

She smiled brightly. "I almost don't have the words to express how grateful I am for everything you've done for me. Thanks to your support I feel like I can conquer the world! It's not just that I've found my mojo again. I feel excited about the future. It's like there's nothing I can't do. Heck, it's not that I feel like my old self again. I feel like I'm *better* than my old self! It's so good to know I'll never have to worry about being burnt out again."

When you're in the throes of burnout, it's almost impossible to see a way out. The future looks like it can only go even further downhill. It's all you can do to focus on putting one foot in front of the other. Unfortunately, all this means is you can only see what's not working - your fatigue, your inability to do what you want to do.

So the first step towards recovery is to start thinking about who you would be without the burnout. What is your ideal vision of yourself? What's your dream life? What do you want others to think about you - how would they describe this ideal vision to someone else?

You might like to make a list of the people you admire. Who do you look up to as a role model? Elon Musk? Gary Vee? Tony Robbins? Consider what exactly it is you like about them. Is it their seemingly boundless energy? Their positivity? Their bank balance? There's no right or wrong here. It's a useful exercise in figuring out your priorities. As an ambitious go-getter, you'll know all about how important it is to set goals. You can't get past your burnout if you don't know what that will look like for you.

Now consider these different areas of your life. You don't need to write anything down just yet. This is designed to provoke thought and create some mental momentum in a positive direction. Pause on each of the sections below. Let your mind explore each of them carefully. Take enough time that you begin to *feel* those things that are important to you.

What do you want to achieve?

PHYSICAL AND MENTAL HEALTH AND WELLNESS

What does being physically and mentally fit and well look like for you? Remember - there's no one right way of viewing this. It's all about imagining what *your* ideal would be.

Do you want to:

- Feel healthy and overflowing with energy?
- Feel comfortable in your body? Have the confidence to take your clothes off in front of a partner or wear a bikini to the beach?
- Look good?
- Have a fitness routine?

- Feel grounded everyday?
- Feel stress free?
- Be mindful and live more in the present moment?

PERSONAL DEVELOPMENT

What are your personal development goals? What does the next level you look like?

Do you want to:

- Feel like you're fulfilling your potential?
- Be a better person?
- Expand your horizons?
- Improve who you are as a human being?
- Build on your strengths?
- Work on your weaknesses?
- Be more self-aware?
- Feel less triggered by other people and their behavior?

RELATIONSHIPS AND YOUR COMMUNITY

How healthy are your relationships with others? Do you feel like you are part of a community? What improvements do you want to see in this part of your life?

Do you want to:

- Feel like you have a sense of purpose in your life?
- Be more altruistic and get more involved in charity work?
- Connect with others in your community and the world at large?
- Serve others in a meaningful way?
- Help improve others' lives?

CAREER AND LIFESTYLE

Right now, your career may be the last thing you want to think about. You may be feeling like it's responsible for your current situation. But right now we're looking at what your ideal life would look like, which includes your career.

Do you want to:

- Feel like your career is in alignment with your purpose in life?
- Work to live rather than live to work?
- Enjoy life and make the most of the time you have here?
- Look forward to going to work?
- Follow your passions in both work and your free time?

CONNECTION WITH YOUR HIGHER SELF

Whatever your religious or spiritual beliefs, it's important to develop your connection with your Higher Self in whatever way has meaning for you.

Do you want to:

- Feel like you're following a higher calling?
- Bring more spirituality into your life?
- Live a meaningful life?
- Rebuild your connection with God/the Universe/Spirit/your Higher Self?

Having thought about these subjects will help you with this next part of the exercise.

Before you write anything down, take a moment to close your eyes and visualize the person you want to embody. Imagine your ideal self is standing in front of you on a golden surface with light beams all around them. Take your time to 'see' this person in vivid detail. What are you wearing? How are you standing? What is your expression? Interact with your ideal self, and really feel the presence of your ideal self.

When you have exhausted your full mental focus on this exercise, ask yourself:

1. What do you see?
2. What does the ideal you look like?
3. How is the ideal you feeling?
4. What are they doing?
5. Did you feel any of their emotions?
6. What's important to them?

Take as long as you need. This will give you a clearer vision of what you truly want. Remember - the focus should be on what you want, not what you think others want for you.

 As these thoughts fill your mind, capture them in your Workbook. Write without pausing, without too much thinking and without any censorship or judgment. Pour out your thoughts as they come to you.

With this exercise complete, you have a vision of where you want to be. Next it's time to build a plan to get you there. That's exactly what we're going to do in the next chapter.

4

YOUR PATH TO RECOVERY

What To Focus On To Conquer Your Burnout

I actually think burnout is the wrong description of it. I think it's burn up. Physiologically, that is what you are doing because of the chronic stress being placed on your body.

– Richard Boyatizis

"How am I meant to get past this, Deanna?" Shelly asked. Tears pricked at the corners of her eyes, as she fidgeted nervously, playing with the hem of her shirt. "I can barely get out of bed in the morning and I'm supposed to be running a huge marketing campaign? People are looking up to me to tell them what to do. I can barely figure out what *I'm* supposed to do!"

"I've been where you are," I told her. "It's tough."

"I went to the doctor, but he just wanted to give me antidepressants," she said. "But I'm not depressed!"

"Adrenal fatigue can explain all your symptoms," I said. "It sounds like you're in late phase adrenal fatigue. Unfortunately, a lot of doctors don't recognize it. But my research has shown that it explains how you're feeling - low mood, irritability, utter exhaustion, a feeling of complete helplessness, brain fog, panic attacks, even existential crises."

"That's exactly it," Shelly said. "That's how I'm feeling *all* the time. But what can I do about it?"

What indeed?

This book is going to give you practical action steps you can take to turn things around in as little as 30 days. That might seem like an impossible goal right now, but it *is* possible. I've done it myself, as have many of my clients.

This transformation occurs through the synergistic force of focusing on these areas:

- Mindset
- Physical health
- Lifestyle

The rest of this book is laid out in the same order as above. Each chapter will break down how the body works in relation to that specific area and explain why it's out of sync. I encourage you to pay attention to this explanation rather than skip over it to the practical tips. This will give context to all my advice so you can understand why you need to do certain things even though they may not initially make sense to you.

YOUR PLAN TO CONQUER BURNOUT

The plan I outline in this book can be completed in as little as 30 days, but if you feel you need to spend more time on any stage, slow down. Don't put pressure on yourself to push forward when you're already feeling under pressure in other areas of your life.

There are just three things you need to remember each day as you complete your transformation:

1. Revisit that feeling you had when you were visualizing yourself as your ideal self. Your subconscious doesn't know the difference between real and vividly imagined. The more you can flood your mind with those positive emotions, the more you'll be able to move forward to the next step.

2. Focus on your daily tasks. Avoid the temptation to think about how slow (or fast) your progress is or what you've got to do later that day. Keep your mind on the step you're

taking on that specific day. Little steps every day will all mount up to a lot of progress.

3. Live in the moment and stay present as much as possible. There's no point in obsessing over the past. You can't change it. Worrying about the future won't make any difference to the outcome. Be here, now - it's all any of us have.

Every day you'll be given a maximum of four <u>new</u> activities. This transformation process is designed to help you reconnect with yourself and undo the damage of adrenal fatigue. It's a cumulative program. Everything you do will add up as you work through them. It's important you don't pick up one thing but drop another.

This process is not about being perfect. Release any pressure on yourself to perform or achieve arbitrary goals. This is all about building habits, staying consistent, and practicing the little things every day so they become second nature.

I warn you now - you will find excuses not to do these tasks! It's up to you to prioritize your mental and physical health. You matter. It's time to give yourself the same level of importance you've been giving everything else. Block off time in your calendar to do your daily tasks and make your self-care time non-negotiable.

You've made a commitment to yourself to tackle your burnout. It's why you picked up this book. In the next chapter, it's time to start the work. We're going to start with where it all began - in your mind.

PART 1

The Mind

Everything starts with a thought. Your journey to recovery begins by getting a clear vision of where you want to go and a roadmap to get there.

5

YOUR THOUGHTS CAN HEAL YOU

The Surprising Ways Your Mindset Affects Your Physical Body

Burnout is so hard to get out of because when you're in it, you ask yourself, 'What can I do to bring me relief from all this pressure and stress of all this work I need to do?' And the only answer you can think of is, 'The only thing that will bring me relief is if I finish this work.'

– Jonny Sun

"I find my mind going round and round in circles," Mike told me in our first session together. "I keep thinking that if I can just get through this project, heck, just write this letter, I'll feel better, but I don't. I feel worse. I know I'm letting everyone down, but I don't know what to do about it."

"What do you mean, you know you're letting everyone down?"

"You know, everyone. My colleagues, my family… If I don't get my work done, it affects my co-workers because they have to pick up my slack. If I lose my job, I won't be able to provide for my family. And my mom was so proud when she heard I'd been promoted. I don't want to let her down."

"That's all important, but what do *you* want?"

The moment I asked the question, I could see a wall crumble. Mike looked like he was about to cry, but he fought back his emotions.

"It's great that you care so much about other people, but I invite you to shift your thinking," I gently continued. "From an early age, we get programmed by society to conform. We think we've got to buy into the 'hustle culture' to prove our worth. We believe that if we aren't shedding blood, sweat and tears we're somehow inferior."

"Yeah, I can relate." Mike sighed.

"Our minds influence every single choice we make," I said. "It shapes what we think is the best way to accomplish our goals. But what if there's a better way? What if we took some time to think about what *we* wanted and set aside any pressure or expectations from society? How would that look for you?"

Mike sat back in his chair. "Sheesh. I have no idea."

THE POWER OF YOUR MIND

Everything starts with a thought. Every action is driven by an idea we have, regardless of whether we're aware of it or not.

It's normal to feel depressed or anxious when you're feeling stressed. However, while some people are able to recover from this when the stress is relieved, others go on to develop a mood disorder. Those who are able to go through stress without it causing a long-term negative emotional effect are thought of as stress-resilient. But what makes one person stress-resilient and not another?

THE ANSWER SEEMS TO LIE IN THE GUT

We will be looking more at gut health in the second part of this book. For now, I'll just give you a little bit of background information so you understand why I'm making the recommendations I am. It has been discovered that gut microbiota are associated with psychological stress-induced issues in the intestinal and blood-brain barriers.[1] During times of stress, the gut microbiota changes, impacting the integrity of the intestinal barrier and blood-brain barrier. These supply the nervous system with information about what's currently happening so you can prepare for a fight-or-flight response. When placed under enough stress, this change can set in for the long-term, even engendering post-traumatic stress symptoms.[2] It would appear that the microbiome-gut-brain axis is key to understanding the causes of burnout.

When we start digging into this subject, your burnout symptoms all start to make sense. For example, many people suffering from burnout find themselves putting on weight without knowing why. Research is starting to show that chronic stress is a major contributor to the development of metabolic disease.[3] In fact, it can even alter your adipose tissue metabolism, contributing to endocrine changes which have an even greater negative effect on the whole-body energy balance.[4]

THE CONNECTION BETWEEN BRAIN HEALTH AND BURNOUT

Our bodies are finely tuned and balanced machines. When one part is out of alignment, it throws everything else off. So this is why this book takes a systemized approach to tackle all the contributing factors of your burnout. If you've tried and failed to treat your burnout because you've been following recommendations you've found on the internet, the reason why they haven't worked is because they only deal with one issue. You need to work on all of them, in a holistic approach. However, since it would be overwhelming to you - and your systems - to deal with them all at the same time, we start with your mindset. Once you have your mind focused in the right direction, it's easier to find the motivation to implement the rest of the recommendations. As you probably know, the human brain is the control center for the entire nervous system. It is responsible for your thoughts, memory, movement, and emotions. It has evolved to be able to process complex functions and place human beings at the top of the evolutionary ladder. If you want to live a long, healthy life, you'll need a healthy brain.

There are three main areas of brain function:

- The interpretation of sensory input and the control of movement
- The maintenance of cognitive, mental, and emotional processes
- The maintenance of normal behavior and social cognition.

A healthy mindset means your moods are predictable and you have a full understanding of why your mood changes through the day, week, year. You should have identified your triggers and know why you respond the way you do so you can consciously react in positive ways. This doesn't mean you need to be happy all the time - that misunderstanding leads to toxic positivity which will result in you feeling even worse. We're all human and life has its ups and downs. When you're in a difficult situation, it's natural to respond with sadness or anger. But a healthy mindset will process these emotions and be able to move past them appropriately rather than remaining in a depressed state.

In addition, a healthy mindset means you have the ability to shift perspectives. You can see things from multiple points of view rather than just your own. You're mentally clear most of the time and have the ability to think and process intentional thoughts.

Understanding the specific causes and areas associated with a mindset that leads to burnout and keeps you there goes a long way towards beating burnout. While overwork can be a contributing factor, the real reasons why you become burnt out run much deeper. These can include:

Feeling out of control, either in your job or in your life in general. If you feel like you don't have the ability to make basic decisions such as setting your schedule, assignments, or workload, or you don't have the resources you need to get things done, this might lead to burnout.

Unclear expectations. If you don't know what others expect from you or you don't know how much authority you have in any given situation, it can leave you feeling uncomfortable or unsettled.

Dysfunctional dynamics at home or in the workplace. Maybe you're being bullied at work or nagged at home. All of this can make you feel chronically stressed.

Extremes in activity levels. If you're engaged in tasks which are monotonous or unpredictable, you'll need to expend a lot of energy to stay focused, which can make you feel fatigued and burned out.

Lack of social support. If you feel isolated and alone at work or in your personal life, this can add to the pressure you're under.

Work-life imbalance. If you're giving so much to your job that you don't have time or energy for your friends and family, you can easily become burned out.

A disconnect between your unconscious needs and the demands of your workplace. For example, if you're an extrovert who loves to build meaningful connections with people, but you're working a job which is mainly solitary with little opportunity for social outlets, you may struggle. Likewise, if you've been promoted to a managerial role but don't like leading, this is going to cause problems.

However you've arrived where you are, your mind can lead you out. So, let's equip your mind with the thoughts and the health it needs to become an ally of yours, not the enemy,

USING YOUR THETA STATE TO REPROGRAM YOUR MIND

You are not your thoughts. You have the power to change your thoughts at any time, replacing negative patterns with more positive, self-affirming ones. When you work with your brain's natural rhythms, it becomes easier to reprogram it. You can take advantage of the specific states when the brain is more open to suggestion to start thinking in a way which supports you rather than undermines you.

The brain is an electrochemical organ. It has been hypothesized that a healthy brain can generate up to 10 watts of electrical power.[5] Its electrical activity is displayed as brainwaves. We'll discuss four categories of these brainwaves:

> **Beta waves** are fast with a low amplitude. Their frequency ranges from 15-40 cycles a second. These brain waves occur when the mind is highly engaged, such as when someone is involved in a conversation or giving a speech.
>
> **Alpha waves** are slower with a higher amplitude. Their frequency ranges from 9-14 cycles a second. Someone

taking time out to rest, reflect, or meditate is generally in an alpha state.

Theta waves are of an even higher amplitude and slower frequency of between 5-8 cycles a second. Someone daydreaming is in a theta state. This state is associated with flashes of insight and inspiration.

Delta waves have the highest amplitude and slowest frequency of around 1.5-4 cycles a second. A deep, dreamless sleep puts you in this low frequency.

So when you go to bed and start to unwind before going to sleep, you'll be in beta. As you close your eyes and drift off, you'll descend through to alpha, theta, and then delta when you're fully asleep.

The theta state is the one we're going to focus on in terms of dealing with your burnout. We usually think about the same things everyday from the moment we wake until we go to sleep. Only a small percentage of our thoughts are actively, consciously created in the present moment.

So when we wake up in the morning, your brain goes from the deep sleep state of delta to theta waves, that beautiful daydream state, before moving on to alpha waves when you're awake but still relaxed and not really processing information.

If you're stressed, you're usually thinking about the same things - *why am I still so tired? I need a coffee. What have I got to deal with today?* You may grab your phone and start digging into what you've got to do and catching up with what you missed while you were asleep. This prematurely forces your body to miss out on the theta and alpha stages and skip straight to the beta state where you're wide awake. **This puts the body into a stress response before the day has even started,** which is going to take its toll on our mental, physical and emotional health.

When you don't spend this important time in the theta state, you're missing an opportunity to heal. Your body has natural systems in place that allow it to repair itself on an ongoing basis. If you stop those systems from working, even unconsciously, you continue to cause yourself harm and make it difficult to recover from burnout, no matter how hard you try.

Fortunately, it's a straightforward process to change how you've been doing things. You can consciously go into this deep level of relaxation. When you do, you leave the fight-or-flight response behind and enter into a parasympathetic nervous system state where your body's systems relax enough to promote deep healing. The relaxed effect of being in theta can last for days, but when you're caught up in the busyness of modern living, it's difficult to go into a theta state.

In your Workbook you'll find simple exercises which will help you utilize the theta state to reprogram your mind and enhance your brain health. The beautiful thing about this is that since our brains naturally enter into a theta state, you're not trying to do something weird or strange. This is a familiar way of being for the mind. You've been experiencing the theta state your whole life.

But what you may not have been aware of is that you can harness the power of the theta state to consciously direct your brain in a healthier fashion. What you're going to do now is intentionally induce a theta state to support a healthy mindset.

For example, meditation is one way of consciously entering into a theta state whereby you can become more aware of limiting beliefs and negative thought patterns and start shifting them in a more supportive direction.

You can also use those thoughts you have first thing in the morning to set intentions for the day. You can choose to set yourself up for positive experiences, feel more patient with people who frustrate you and prioritize what's important for the day.

When you first wake up, before you reach for your phone, before you do *anything*, with your eyes closed, take a few moments to focus on your breath. Watch as it flows in and out without trying to control it in any way. Notice how your breath continues to move without you having to make any effort. It just is.

Now as you inhale, silently say to yourself, *I am worthy.* Exhale and send away any doubts about that statement.

With your next inhale say to yourself, *I am healthy.* Exhale and send away any doubts about that statement.

With your next inhale say to yourself, *I am going to have a good day.* Exhale and send away any doubts about that statement.

Congratulations! You've just done a simple meditation *and* you've programmed your mind to start the day with a positive mindset.

Again, you'll find more about this process and additional exercises in your Workbook.

YOUR LIMITING BELIEFS AND HOW THEY KEEP YOU BURNT OUT

A limiting belief is a story we tell ourselves which holds us back from stepping into our true authentic self. If something isn't universally true for everyone, it's a limiting belief, a story you can rewrite for a more empowered life. Our limiting beliefs are often buried so deeply in our subconscious that we don't even know we have them until someone tells us. This is why taking time out to truthfully examine our tendencies and beliefs can help us see how our mindset has been holding us back so we can do something to change it.

The human brain uses a huge amount of your energy but wants to use it as efficiently as possible. This is why we look for predictability in our routines, relationships, and jobs. We stay in our comfort zones, which may not be all that comfortable but certainly keep us safe. We only pour energy into taking action if we think it will generate a result. If we don't think we can get a result - because a limiting belief tells us so - we don't bother. We self-sabotage our success and then point the finger at anything but ourselves.

Limiting beliefs impact every aspect of our lives. Common examples include:

> **"I don't have time"** Which is unlikely when you analyze it, because we all seem to have plenty of time for scrolling on social media! If something seems important enough, we make time for it. We all have a lot more choice over what we do with the 24 hours in a day than we tell ourselves.

"I'm not good enough". We often tell ourselves we can't achieve what we want because we don't have the skills. But imagine what you *could* accomplish if you poured the same energy you currently use to hold yourself back into learning those new skills.

"I can't cope with failure". This limiting belief convinces us that we don't have the fortitude to deal with rejection or failure. It's easier to not try something new than it is to try and fail. Yet it's those failures which teach us so much and help us get to the next level.

"I'm not worthy of love". So many of us believe this and it has a devastating effect on our relationships. It keeps us from finding the perfect partner and sabotages our hopes of a healthy relationship by causing arguments, making someone cheat, or completely give up on finding love.

These limiting beliefs can be formed from a very early age, which is why we're frequently unaware of them. They may come because someone told us something, such as a parent or authority figure. They may develop because you observed behaviors and thought they represented a universal truth. Or you may simply decide to believe something because it's easier than dealing with reality or daring to try and risk failure.

When you start to identify your limiting beliefs, ask yourself, *is this true or is it just a story I tell myself?* If you can think of any exceptions, even if it's only one, then it's a story. And the great thing about stories is that you can always write new ones.

YOUR RECOVERY JOURNEY

Your Workbook contains activities to help you discover your own limiting beliefs. Go to your Workbook now and you'll be prompted to consider your own beliefs, where they originated and how they influence you today.

Once you've completed those activities, I'd invite you to commence the 30-Day Program that I have included in the back of the Workbook.

The activities included in this 30-Day program are the same ones that I invite my clients to do when they are working directly with me. Should you choose to follow along with these steps, it's as close as we can get to working directly with each other. And, based on the experiences of hundreds of clients before you, I know that if you do follow these steps, your recovery will happen ... and it will be life-changing!

In the Workbook you'll be invited to start your journey with the activities for Day 0. These activities relate to what you've read so far. The next day you'll move along to Day 1 and continue throughout the 30 days.

 Get your recovery started today. Get your copy of the Workbook at: www.learnwellbooks.com/alive

Now is also a good time to join the LearnWell Community if you haven't already.

6

CHANGE YOUR MIND, CHANGE YOUR LIFE

Six Steps To Reprogram Your Limiting Beliefs For A More Fulfilling Life

Gratitude for everything you still have, and every step of your recovery, is such an important part of healing from burnout.

– Emma Matthews

There's a story which circulates the internet about an experiment involving five monkeys, a banana and a ladder. Scientists put the monkeys in a room with a banana suspended in the middle from the ceiling. There was a ladder beneath the banana. All the monkeys had to do was climb the ladder to get the banana. However, as soon as one monkey started to climb the ladder, the remaining monkeys were given an electric shock.

This happened every time a monkey tried to get to the banana until they all gave up trying. None of them went anywhere near the ladder.

When this happened, the scientists switched out one of the monkeys with a new monkey. Naturally, the new monkey went straight for the banana, but the other four monkeys immediately attacked him, stopping him from going up the ladder. Every time the new monkey tried to get to the banana, the others attacked him, so eventually he stopped trying.

As soon as the monkey stopped trying to get to the banana, the scientists replaced another of the original monkeys with a new monkey. Again, this monkey tried to get to the banana only to have the other monkeys attack him if he attempted to go anywhere near the ladder.

And so it went on until none of the original monkeys were in the room. None of the remaining monkeys had ever received an electric shock. In fact, the equipment used to deliver the shocks had long since been removed, yet they refused to go anywhere near the ladder. None of the monkeys ever did get to enjoy the banana.

This is the power of a limiting belief.

Limiting beliefs are what hold us back from living the life we want. They're insidious and sneaky. What's more, most of us are unaware we have certain beliefs. Unless it's a strong, polarizing opinion, most of the time, our beliefs remain unchallenged. We accept our beliefs as objective fact instead of their true nature - a story we tell ourselves. Nothing more, nothing less.

Since we're so unaware of our beliefs, this limiting aspect of them is taken as true by our subconscious, which can potentially lead to a lifetime of living in the confinement of an invisible box. We become just like the monkeys in the experiment. We refuse to climb the ladder that could lead us out of our current situation because we believe something terrible will happen.

When we start becoming aware of our limiting beliefs, we can recognize, resolve, and reprogram them. I'm going to take you through a six-step process which will enable you to identify and brainstorm your current belief system about these critical areas of your life:

- Your physical and mental health
- Personal development
- Your career and lifestyle
- Relationships

STEP 1 - YOUR THOUGHT JOURNAL

Keep your Workbook close. It's a regular companion to this text. In it you'll find activities that will support what you read. Speaking of which ... turn to your Workbook now where you'll find the following prompts and space to write underneath them.

Whenever you think or say the following, write down the context and area of focus *without* recording the prompt:

- I can't...
- I don't have...
- I will never...
- What if...
- If only...
- I wish...

When you're noting these down, **only** record the context and area of focus. For example, if you notice yourself saying, "I don't have time to go to the gym," write down *training/going to the gym* rather than the complete sentence.

STEP 2 - TRACE THAT THOUGHT TO ITS ORIGIN

Building on the example above, as you start documenting your thoughts, you may realize you've been telling yourself you don't have time to go to the gym 1-2 times a week. So ask yourself, *what do I do during the time I plan to workout?* You may discover that you're usually working instead.

Ask yourself why. It may be you're trying to get as much done as possible so you feel productive and as though you've achieved something.

Ask yourself, *where does this association of constantly working equates to being productive come from?* You may remember that your parents told you from an early age that you needed to work hard to make money so you could be someone, feel like you're worthy of taking up space in this world.

A-ha! Now we're getting somewhere.

STEP 3 - RECOGNIZE YOUR LIMITING BELIEF

Now we know that the reason why you're avoiding the gym has got nothing to do with not wanting to work out. It's all to do with a need to feel worthy. So in this example, the actual limiting belief would be *My worthiness is dependent upon my busyness and the monetary success I obtain.*

STEP 4 - DISCOVER WHETHER THIS LIMITING BELIEF IS TRUE

A belief can form as a statement which gets repeated over and over until it becomes second nature. Your mind resorts to it on autopilot. By slowing down and questioning the nature of the statement - whether or not it's true - you're pausing the automated process of filtering your experiences through this belief when interpreting your reality.

In this instance, asking yourself *is my worthiness dependent upon my busyness and the monetary success I obtain?* might sound silly and nonsensical when you put it out in the open. You're bringing it up to your conscious mind where you can shine a light on it rather than allowing it to operate at a subconscious level. But it's important to look at it to determine whether it's objectively true.

If you've asked the question and decided that it's true, pause and ask yourself:

- Do I have to be busy and rich for my loved ones to love me (my parents, kids, friends, spouse, etc.)?
- Other than being productive and rich, what other activities/areas bring me true joy?
- If I were to leave this Earth tomorrow, what would I miss?

Chances are, after asking yourself these questions you'll realize that this statement isn't true.

If you can recognize this statement is false, move on to step five.

STEP 5 - CHANGE THIS LIMITING BELIEF TO A SUPPORTIVE STATEMENT WHICH SUPPORTS THE LIFE YOU WANT TO LIVE

It's really hard to change a belief you've been carrying for a long time. But hard isn't impossible. Like words etched into a rock, it'll take a bit of work to remove, but you *can* remove it. In this step, you're going to reframe the old belief into a statement that supports the life you want to live, one filled with abundance, love, freedom, happiness... whatever you want. You're going to reframe your limiting belief to support your new life.

Let's say you want to feel free and empowered by your decisions. You might take the limiting belief *My worthiness is dependent on my busyness and the monetary success I obtain* and reframe it so it becomes:

My definition of success is time freedom, spending time with people I love, and feeling true happiness regardless of the outcome of my work.

My productivity means efficiency and effectiveness, not the number of hours I pour into my work.

My worthiness comes from within - my quality of thoughts, my health, happiness, and how I treat those around me.

STEP 6 - YOUR POWER STATEMENT

A belief is just a statement until it becomes automatic. So let's turn those 3 sentences into a concise, to-the-point statement you can repeat and easily program into your brain.

Your power statement might be

I am worthy regardless of my external circumstances or my performance. My worthiness comes from within. I choose to be worthy.

Remember, it's important to repeat your power statement regularly, ideally every day. Since your limiting belief was simply a neutral statement repeated until it became a belief system for you. In order for you to replace it with something else, that new statement needs to be repeated in place of the old statement.

There is space in your Workbook to write down, read and re-read your power statement

Everything we do is to chase a feeling, regardless of whether that's a good or bad thing. It's time to start giving serious consideration to where your decisions are coming from.

The three basic human needs are safety, control, and approval. Any one of these can drive you to burnout if they're taken to an extreme. Start consciously questioning what you're trying to achieve when you work yourself to this point. Determining which of the core needs are driving a surface level desire, you become more adept at getting what you really want. You can respond more effectively to the people and situations around you.

Our need for **safety** is tied to the instinct to survive. It's the most basic of the core needs. We want to stay alive and avoid death for as long as possible. From this need to stay safe comes a desire for security on every level - financial, occupational, material, relational, etc.

Our need for **approval** comes about because humans are naturally social creatures who want to belong. We want to be desired, liked, wanted, appreciated, valued, and feel like we belong to something greater than ourselves. Again, this ties back to the urge to survive - from an evolutionary perspective, we believe that if others approve of us they won't kill us.

Our need for **control** is another way to gain security. If you can't gain approval from someone, an alternative is to control them so they won't hurt you. Trying to control your life means you attempt to get everything to go the way you want. You can try to control yourself, the people around you, your situation, and the opportunities which come your way.

As an example of how these core needs show up in our regular wishes and desires, let's say you want to get a promotion. Your reasons for this might be:

- I want to make more money to be able to provide for my family. (Security.)
- I want greater influence over my department so we can bring my vision to life. (Control.)
- I want the respect of others in my industry. (Approval.)

IT'S TIME TO TAKE INVENTORY

Let's look at the life you're currently living vs the life you want to live by asking yourself the following questions. You'll find these repeated in your Workbook with space to write your responses:

- On a scale of 0-10, 10 being absolutely satisfied and 0 being hating it, how would you rate the following areas in your current life:
  - Career/job satisfaction
  - Relationships
  - Overall happiness

- Physical and mental health
- Where you are currently in life
- Your lifestyle
- Overall quality of life
- If money wasn't an issue, what would you be doing right now? (If you answered something other than your current job/career, is it something you'll eventually get to through your job/career?)
- How much longer can you go with your current stress level if it doesn't get addressed?
- If you've been feeling subpar in your mental and/or physical performance, how much longer can you go if the issues don't get resolved?
- If your life ends tomorrow, how would others remember you? How would you remember yourself?
- Did you ever have a different image of how your life would unfold? If yes, what was it?
- What makes you truly happy? What puts a smile on your face, makes your heart warm, and feels like you love life so freaking much?
- If you were given a chance to choose how you'd live the rest of your life, what would you choose?
- Close your eyes. What does your perfect life look like?

In the previous chapter we learned how our brains experience different brain waves during different activities. Studies have shown that the average person spends about 47% of their time on autopilot.[1] If you've ever zoned out during a conversation or while driving, you were functioning on autopilot. During these times, our actions are driven by the thoughts and habits we've repeatedly practiced. Even if we're not zoned out, we often act first in accordance with our autopilot and think about it or regret it later.

If we want to change our thoughts and habits, we need to consciously engage our mind.

Our autopilot runs on theta brainwaves. We wake up in a theta state, which is why we usually wake up to the same old thoughts every day. If we can reprogram these thoughts, we can start shifting the way we think, act, and respond.

Here are four simple ways you can get off autopilot and live with purpose starting right now:

1. Set an intention for your day every morning. This is like programming a destination into your GPS. It gives you a sense of direction, something to aim at.

2. Start the day by listing the feelings you'd like to experience within the next 24 hours such as joy, calm, abundance, etc. Schedule at least 2 activities which support those feelings.

3. Change how you do things at least once a day. For example, if you tend to take Main Street to work every morning, take King Street instead. Changing your habits/routine will give you a fresh perspective and activate the brain to pay more attention.

4. Connect with mother nature. This is a way to connect with yourself. We're all part of the natural world. Taking at least 15 minutes a day to walk by the water, on the beach, in the forest, or even in a park will shift your brain chemistry and the hormonal balance within your body. You'll feel the ease of becoming present and a rush of gratitude.

IT'S ALWAYS BEEN INSIDE

Earlier in this book we did an exercise where you visualized your ideal self. We're going to build on that now so you can understand that the person you want to be is already here.

Close your eyes and visualize the ideal you standing in front of you, the person you want to embody. If it helps, go back to your notes in Chapter 2. Visualize yourself walking toward that person, step by step. With every step you take you feel more confident, loved, whole, and more like your ideal self. As you reach your ideal self, realize you have become them. You *are* your ideal self. Take a few minutes to embrace this feeling and live in this body which you feel so confident in. Exist in a state where you're feeling exactly how you want to feel.

When you're ready, write down the answers to the following questions in your Workbook:

- What does your ideal self feel like?
- Did you feel something new? Something you've never experienced before?

- As you left the exercise and returned to your present-day self, were there feelings you left behind?

- If you could feel like your ideal self for the rest of your life, would you?

If you've started your 30-Day Program, you'll also find some related and thought-provoking activities in Days 3, 4 and 5.

7

DO LESS, GET MORE

Five Steps To Replacing Your Bad Habits With Positive Ones

*In dealing with those who are undergoing great suffering, if you feel 'burnout' setting in, if you feel demoralized and exhausted, it is best, for the sake of everyone, to withdraw and restore yourself.
The point is to have a long-term perspective.*

– Dalai Lama

"I've been doing everything I can think of to improve things, but nothing's worked." A new client was sitting opposite me. Smartly dressed in a suit and tie, Craig was perched on the edge of his seat as if he wanted to run out of the room at any moment. "I've Googled, meditated, you name it. I just end up feeling worse than before!"

"When you say everything, what do you mean?"

"Well, I try to multitask, you know, work smarter, not harder, but I end up falling further behind. I try to take time out, but I've got so much to do, I'd rather get work done than have some downtime. I've got a good routine. I know I do. It's worked for me for years. I just don't get why I feel like I'm falling apart now." He caught himself. "Although I suppose if I had more help from the people around me, maybe I wouldn't have to work so hard. Nobody seems to care about the job as much as I do."

"Have you considered whether maybe it's your routine that is the problem?"

He frowned. "What do you mean?"

"Well, we all develop habits over time. Some of these are good habits, like brushing our hair or having a shower in the morning. But other habits aren't so great. Not allowing ourselves time to rest and recuperate, trying to do everything, heck, even our attitudes can be a bad habit."

"So are you saying it's my habits that have got me here?"

"Partly." I nodded. "And the great thing about that is that you can always replace habits which no longer serve you with more positive ones. Are you up for doing that?"

"If it'll get me out of this rut, I'm all for it."

Habits are a natural part of human nature. In the previous chapters we've looked at the importance of mindset. Now it's time to dig even deeper to examine our habits and how we need to shift those patterns of behavior to instill healthier habits.

WHAT ARE HABITS?

Habits are automatic behaviors developed through repetition. This repetition creates a mental link between a situation and an action or behavior. This can lead to so-called habit loops which follow this formula: there's a trigger, which sets off an associated behavior which gives you a result or reward. This reward may not be in our best interest, but at some point it served us.

Let's take smoking as an example. You may experience stress (the trigger), which makes you reach for a cigarette (the behavior). Smoking that cigarette temporarily relieves that stress (the reward). Our brains recognize that the behavior of smoking helps deal with the trigger, so the reward is enough for our brain to decide to do it again.

Unfortunately, smoking a cigarette doesn't deal with the root cause of the stress. You'll still have to deal with whatever it was that was making you stressed - a difficult family member, demanding boss, challenging work environment, etc. But rather than tackling the issue, the habit is formed.

Habits have nothing to do with willpower or self-control. They are simply a result of this trigger → behavior → reward process programming our brains to respond in a particular way in certain circumstances.

THE FOUR MAIN TYPES OF HABITS

> **Habits of wanting.** These are associated with getting something we desire, which could be drink, drugs, food, cigarettes, food, or anything else we crave. Our feelings of wellbeing and happiness become intertwined with that thing, regardless of whether it's actually good for us.
>
> **Habits of distraction.** These are ways in which you distract yourself, say, by watching TV or scrolling through social media. Anything to take your mind off what's really troubling you.
>
> **Habits of resistance.** These habits display in our behavior. We may act frustrated, annoyed, impatient, angry, or other ways which we defend ourselves from perceived threats, regardless of whether they're real or not.
>
> **Habits of doing.** These habits give us the feeling we need to keep active, that something bad will happen if we don't keep making things happen. This is often a habit many burned out people develop - this drive to keep busy is almost irresistible, even though it is pushing you into burnout.

WHAT ARE _YOUR_ HABITS?

What habits have you created? Do they serve you? Are there some habits you'd like to replace?

It's time for a stocktake. Pause for a moment to consider a day in the life of you. What habits run your day, your attitude, your behavior and your outcomes? Make a list of ALL your habits, you can then take the role of deciding which ones you'd like to keep and which you'd like to break.

You'll find space in your Workbook for your habit stocktake. Go there now and make the list. It's a powerful exercise and I know you'll be amazed at what you discover!

Then, when it's time to break some habits, how do we do that? By replacing them with new ones.

ESTABLISHING NEW HABITS

Have you heard the saying that it takes 21 days to form a new habit? And did you know that it's not true? In fact, it takes more like an average of 66 days to establish a new habit (just over two months), but it can take anything up to 254 days. That might sound like a long time, but when you understand that it's going to take a while for your new healthy habits to kick in, you'll be able to be patient with yourself.

One of the reasons why you've struggled to overcome your burnout is likely to have been unrealistic expectations. Not understanding what really goes into changing established habits means you don't know what's normal and what's not. Therefore, you give up before you've really had a chance to get started.

These are some of the most common mistakes I see in my clients when they've been trying to set up a new habit:

Trying to change too many habits at once. When you overburden yourself with multiple changes at the same time, you're setting yourself up for failure. You'll then feel disappointed in yourself and struggle to find the motivation to try again. Change one habit at a time. Gradual change will enable you to build lifelong habits rather than being 'good' for a few weeks and then quitting.

Being too ambitious. It's great to have big goals, but break them down into little steps and start small. For example, if you want to get fit, rather than immediately cleaning up your diet and spending two hours at the gym every day, start by increasing the amount of fruit and vegetables you eat and make a commitment to go to the gym three days a week. Once you're comfortable with that routine, you can build on it. Make it as tiny and easy as you can, so it's impossible for you to say no to doing it.

Being inconsistent. These new habits are going to take time. Often, people decide it's too difficult and they're not ready to change. If you're serious about getting over your burnout, you'll need to be patient.

Lacking focus. We're bombarded with distractions all the time. There's always going to be something which comes up to take your attention away from where it should be. Notifications will ping, your phone will ring. Your mind will start wandering to all those things on your to-do list. Keep your focus on where it needs to be and deal with those distractions later.

Not understanding that little steps add up. As I mentioned above, start small. If you want to get in shape, you could do just one push up a day. Over time, that push up will help you build strength and do two push ups, three, more. But when these steps seem too small, it's hard to see the difference they make. Us overachievers want results yesterday! So those little steps start to seem pointless so we stop before they've had a chance to have an effect.

Not knowing your 'why.' What's the reason you started this process? The real reason? It's important you understand your motivation for doing this because that's what will help you push through procrastination and ignore distractions.

Wanting results too soon. I get it. You're done with feeling burned out. You want to see progress immediately. But it doesn't work like that. These changes are subtle. Let go of expecting a particular result at a particular time. Focus on the process and let the rest come to you when the time is right.

Giving up after one setback. When things aren't working straight away, it's easy to decide that it's not working at all, so you give up. But every failure is a learning process. You're bound to make a few mistakes and drop the ball when you're developing new habits. It's perfectly normal. The important thing is that you pick yourself up and keep going. Don't give up. Doing something different is the only way you can make a change.

FIVE STEPS TO ESTABLISHING NEW HABITS

Step 1: Decide On The Habit You Want To Form And Why You're Forming It

If you've been following the program in this book, you'll know what you're getting out of this process. You'll have visualized the person you want to be once you've conquered your burnout. Be absolutely clear with yourself about your end goal. Humans love results, especially results we can measure and see.

Accept that results will not come right away. You will fail along the way. There will be days when you're tempted to go back to old habits because the new habits don't seem to be making any difference. It's like when you decide to lose weight. You usually only start seeing visible physical results at the third or fourth week. At the beginning it seems like everything you're doing is pointless and that extra piece of cake won't sabotage your progress. Letting yourself regularly make exceptions is a slippery slope which will take you right back to where you started.

Step 2: Plan It Out And Slot It In

Once you've made time in your calendar for your new habits, it's non-negotiable. No ifs or buts. Decide to do your new habit at the same time everyday and pair it with something you already do daily. For example, if you always forget to take your supplements at night, do it right after you brush your teeth. Brushing your teeth becomes the trigger for you to take supplements as a paired habit.

Step 3: Present The Carrot

We all love rewards. You'll have received them from early childhood when you got brownie points or gold stars. Put in place an instant reward system for completing a habit.

For example, whenever you brush your teeth (the trigger) and take your supplements (the paired habit), you could put some money into a jar or account to save towards something you really want but can't justify buying. The prize at the end will reward your consistency and make the purchase justifiable. After a certain period of time, you won't need the reward to reinforce the habit and you can start rewarding yourself for a new habit.

Step 4: Establish A 'Not Today' Back-Up

We all have days when we try to talk ourselves out of things (I don't need to go to the gym today) or into things (I can have an extra glass of wine). So when you have one of those days, what are you going to do?

Putting in place a strategy for coping with these days will help you be more prepared when you start trying to talk yourself out of sticking with the program. You might like to have an alternative prepared, e.g. instead of going to the gym, you go for a 45 minute walk or run. Or you could write yourself a note reminding your future self why this habit is important to you and how it's contributing to a better future.

Step 5: Visualize

We all create the life we're living. Seeing the successful integration of your new habits on the big screen of your mind is incredibly important. Visualization doesn't just give you the understanding of how you're going to feel when you've established all these new habits, but it will also form actual neuronal connections in the brain as if you've already been doing them.

Top athletes use visualization to help them do better in competitions. They rehearse an event in their mind over and over before they actually compete because it is proven to enhance their performance.

Visualization:

- Strengthens neural connections.

- Positively reinforces habits and actions. (Good feelings means you do more of that same thing so you can feel good about doing it.)

- Is a form of rehearsal, making real life practices easier.

- Helps you know what to expect.[3]

Your Workbook provides space for you to write down all of the new habits you'd like to establish. You'll write them down and then work through the 5-step plan to get them in place.

PART 2

The Body

In the first part of this book we looked at mindset, laying down the foundation for your healing journey. Now we turn to working on your physical health so you can recover from your adrenal fatigue.

PUFFY & BACKED UP

The Shocking Impact Of Acute And Chronic Inflammation

When we train, our performance improves as we adapt to stress. Over time, however, if the stresses are too great or we don't incorporate sufficient recovery time, gains begin to diminish. To grow and adapt, we require stress, but equally we need periods of rest and recovery. This is a delicate balance to strike.

– Chris Duffing

Before I realized I was burnt out, I went to my doctor to see if there was an underlying cause for how I was feeling. He told me my labs and physicals were fine. He suggested I was just depressed and wanted to give me antidepressants, but I knew that wasn't the problem. Unfortunately though, I didn't know what it was. I began to wonder whether it was my busy schedule, even though I'd always been able to perform at a high level in the past. I even questioned whether it was simply that I was getting old.

Even though there were times I doubted my sanity, I kept investigating and eventually arrived at the conclusion that I was chronically inflamed. Good! It meant that there was finally a physical explanation for how I was feeling and I could do something about it. I knew I needed to make a change and I was closer to understanding what that change needed to be.

That's what this section is about. We've done a lot of work on your mind, it's time to move on to the next part of the equation - your body. If you're suffering from burnout, you'll also be suffering from inflammation. This occurs when your body activates your immune system in response to a perceived threat such as viruses, bacteria, chemicals, etc., sending out inflammatory cells. This triggers the inflammation.

There are two main types of inflammation - acute and chronic.

- Acute inflammation is a response to sudden trauma, such as cutting yourself. The inflammatory cells start the healing process to deal with the cut.

- Chronic inflammation is a prolonged state of heightened immune response, characterized by the persistent presence of inflammatory cells and molecules, even in the absence of a clear triggering stimulus.

Chronic inflammation can cause many of the symptoms you will have been experiencing due to burnout, such as fatigue, abdominal pain, chest pain, or stiffness. There is an increasing amount of evidence which suggests that excessive inflammation plays a major role in stress-related diseases, although the mechanism of this has yet to be fully determined.[1]

Constant stress is a known trigger for chronic inflammation. This inflammation can cause a multitude of health issues, including serious conditions such as diabetes and heart disease. Normally, the blood-brain barrier protects your brain from circulating molecules. When placed under chronic stress, this barrier becomes 'leaky', meaning inflammatory proteins can get into the brain. Studies have shown that inflammation can negatively impact brain systems connected to motivation, mental agility, learning, and memory.[2]

Chronic stress also affects the hormones in the brain, such as cortisol and corticotropin releasing factor (CRF). As you read earlier, when levels of cortisol remain high for prolonged periods, this can cause mood disorders and physical problems such as irregular menstrual cycles. In addition, it can interfere with your sleep, making depression and anxiety worse.

DETOXIFICATION

One of the most insidious aspects of burnout is the fact that your body is working against itself. Our bodies are always dealing with toxic substances. These can be in the environment, but normal bodily functions can also generate toxins which need to be detoxified. When your lifestyle is healthy and your systems are all working properly, this detox process happens automatically, flushing out the toxins we come into contact with during our everyday life. If the body becomes overwhelmed, we get the chronic inflammation associated with burnout.

The body has various mechanisms for eliminating toxins:

- The lungs remove gas from the body

- The skin acts as a barrier against toxic substances from the external world and as the largest organ of elimination in the body.

- The digestive system gets rid of toxins through bowel movements. In cases of toxic substances, vomiting and diarrhea are often observed.

- Kidneys secrete toxins or filter them out of the blood into urine.

- The liver detoxifies by altering the chemical nature of certain toxins.

Without all these processes we would constantly be sick. Even in a clean environment, our bodies still generate toxic chemicals.

While the liver is held to be the main organ of detoxification, do not underestimate the importance of the intestinal epithelial barrier – a layer of cells that lines the gut and helps to keep out bad things while letting in good things like nutrients. It's an important part of the gastrointestinal tract, the system that helps the body digest and absorb food. The gastrointestinal tract (GIT) is a major way for the body to deal with toxic substances. During your lifetime the GIT will process over 25 tonnes of food, comprising the largest amount of antigens and toxins the body has to deal with.

Usually, protective mechanisms in the gut support the absorption of nutrients while keeping out potentially harmful substances. But when the intestinal epithelial lining is damaged (sometimes called leaky gut), unwanted molecules can enter the bloodstream, placing an extra burden on the liver. This means that restoring and supporting the integrity and function of the intestinal barrier is an essential part of the detoxification process.

Since the impact of toxins on the body is well documented, it is no surprise that many companies advertise detox plans as being simple and straightforward, a quick fix for whatever ails you.

The reality is that there's no magic bullet that can fix your issues. Your detox organs are waging a constant war against the toxins which would damage your body and most of the time, this process is undetectable. When something goes wrong, it's a different story.

Everybody has different needs when it comes to supporting their body's detoxification process. In your Workbook, you'll find a few suggestions which will help you identify what is most appropriate for you.

DETOX IS A WAY OF LIFE

Just as your heart is always beating and your lungs are always breathing, your body's detoxification processes are always working for you. When these vital systems are functioning optimally, this shows up as good health. You are able to resist any bugs you encounter, you're filled with energy and your sleep patterns are regular and refreshing. If any part of it falls down, your health soon suffers. The early signs of chronic inflammation would have been visible as the early signs of burnout but if you weren't aware of their significance, you probably ignored them and attempted to push through. That's how you got to where you are today.

As you start to put together a detox plan, shift your thinking from this being a detox 'plan' but rather a healthy lifestyle which supports your body in the best way. You'll gain increased self-awareness and understand your body in a way you never have before.

The tactics you use will vary according to what's going on at any given time. In your Workbook, you'll discover ways to help your detox systems. Once you've regained a healthy balance, moving forward, all you'll usually need to do is provide gentle, natural support to specific organs so they can continue to do the job they were designed to do.

Your vital organs are continuously working every single day to keep you alive and healthy. Each one is interrelated and part of a bigger picture that makes up your body's overall health. When you suffer a health problem seemingly unrelated to the detox process, it may well still be affecting one of those organs, impacting their ability to detox your body. Likewise, issues such as skin disorders which seem unconnected to the main internal organs could actually be a sign that your body's detox system's need some extra help.

THE LUNGS

You are detoxing with every breath. You should breathe in and out roughly 15-25 times per minute. Try holding your breath and you'll quickly discover how important your lungs are to life.

If the liver, kidneys and GIT can't eliminate a toxin or break it down to be digested and excreted, the lungs step in to help out. The toxins are taken by the bloodstream to the alveolar sacs at the bottom of the lungs. There, the lungs take them up and cough them out as phlegm.

THE SKIN

The skin forms a barrier which is the body's first line of defense against germs. It also activates your immune system when harmful bacteria get through. It expels toxins from the body while keeping in the beneficial chemicals.

The skin's role is partly to sweat and expel waste by-products from digested foods and remove uric acid and urea. You can encourage your body to sweat out toxins through physical exercise. Getting out of breath and sweaty can promote blood circulation and trigger the process of pushing toxins to the surface of the skin.

When the liver, kidney, and lungs are overwhelmed by toxins, the skin helps out. However, this comes at a price - skin problems. If you find yourself suffering from acne, whiteheads, cysts, rashes, and boils, it's a sign that your detoxification system is overburdened.

THE LIVER

The liver takes on the lion's share of detoxifying the body. It is meant to protect you from toxins in food additives, medicines, drugs, alcohol, and other negative substances while retaining the nutritious foodstuffs which fuel your body.

The liver processes the things you put into your body and breaks them down to their chemical components. It can then distribute the helpful chemicals into the bloodstream while breaking down harmful chemicals to make them ready for excretion. While the liver is not directly responsible for waste excretion, constipation can negatively affect its working. This is because when you are constipated, toxins which should have been excreted stay in the colon where they are reabsorbed. The liver detoxifies them again, using up important energy.

THE KIDNEYS

The kidneys build on the liver's work by filtering the blood, separating out the unnecessary toxins to turn them into urine which can then be excreted. In order to do this, your kidneys rely on you drinking enough water.

If you are fully hydrated, your kidneys will be able to clear out waste and harmful chemicals from your bloodstream, purifying the blood. This filtration process occurs 20-25 times a day. Dehydration can heavily undermine your kidneys' function.

While there are other parts of the body which support the detoxification process, such as the intestines and lymph system, these are the main organs you should focus on. Now you know why fads such as detox months aren't going to counteract the effects of overeating and drinking. This is why although your Workbook guides you through an initial 30 days of your recovery burnout, you need to view this as a permanent lifestyle change, not a quick fix. If you want to conquer your burnout once and for all, you need to commit to doing things differently from now on. What you've been doing up until now is what burned you out. What you're going to do moving forward will free you from burnout for the rest of your life.

In the next chapter, we're going to look at one of the most important parts of the body when it comes to burnout: the gut. We're going to learn all about how good health starts and ends here and how healing your gut can heal your burnout.

9

TRUST YOUR GUT

The Surprising Connection Between Gut Health And Burnout

Quite literally, your gut is the epicenter of your mental and physical health. If you want better immunity, efficient digestion, improved clarity and balance, focus on rebuilding your gut health.

– Kriss Carr

"Can I tell you something a little embarrassing?" Clare, the client sitting in my office, nervously picked at a thumbnail, struggling to meet my eyes.

"Of course," I said warmly, wanting to reassure her. "I promise you there's nothing you can tell me I haven't heard before."

"You know you asked me to detail all the physical symptoms I've been experiencing while I've been feeling burnt out?"

"Yes."

"There's one thing I missed off the list, but I think it's important I tell you everything."

"Absolutely." I nodded. "The more information I have, the better I can support you."

"I've been dealing with digestive problems for as long as I can remember. I've always had really bad flatulence and random nausea. But things have been getting worse recently. I've got almost constant diarrhea. Pretty much anything I eat goes straight through me. I've been losing weight and I really don't think I can afford to lose any more. I've tried seeing a consultant who told me to keep a food diary, but all that's happened is my diet is getting more and more restricted with no change. I've got major acid reflux and my stomach gurgles really loudly."

As if on cue, a loud gurgle came from her stomach. She shrugged sheepishly.

"Do you think this could all be related to my burnout?"

"Definitely," I told her. "Burnout is known to be associated with many digestive issues. Healing your burnout will help with your gut - but healing your gut will also help with your burnout. Thank you for telling me. It means we can be a lot more targeted with your treatment."

Scientists are becoming increasingly aware of the connection between gut health and overall well-being. As Hippocrates said, "Let food be thy medicine." It might have taken modern medicine a while to acknowledge this ancient wisdom, but now it's recognized that healing your gut heals other seemingly unconnected issues.

THE LINK BETWEEN STRESS AND GUT HEALTH

In your Workbook, you'll be asked to reflect without judgment on your diet over the past couple of weeks. With your gut, it really is the case that garbage in, garbage out! However, one person's trash is another person's treasure, so while we can make broad statements about which foods are healthy and which aren't, there will always be individual adjustments that need to be made to eat an appropriate diet to support your gut.

Your enteric (intestinal) nervous system is sometimes called the 'second brain' because it uses the same types of neurons and neurotransmitters found in the central nervous system (brain and spinal cord). When food enters the gut, neurons lining the digestive tract send signals to start peristalsis and the digestive process. However, at the same time, the enteric nervous system is using neurotransmitters, such as serotonin, to communicate and interact with the central nervous system.

This 'brain-gut axis' might explain why stress causes digestive issues. Extreme stress triggers the fight-or-flight response, which causes digestion to slow or even stop so all the body's energy can be directed towards dealing with the threat. Even in less stressful situations, such as needing to give a presentation, these lower levels of stress can impact the digestive process, causing abdominal pain and other GI problems.

Something that is important to bear in mind is that this goes both ways. If you have ongoing GI problems, it can increase anxiety and stress. Whatever way you look at it, it makes sense to improve your gut health.

YOUR GUT AND YOUR HORMONES

Your microbiome (the trillions of bacteria in your GI tract) are critical to a healthy physiology and metabolism. Your gut is intrinsically connected to your overall health and hormone levels.

WHAT IS 'LEAKY GUT'?

Your digestive system is lined with tiny peepholes in the junctions between the gut cells. These gap junctions are tightly regulated in healthy guts to only allow the transportation of water, ions, and certain nutrients to pass from gut to blood.

A damaged gut can mean that these holes will open and stay open, increasing the gut permeability. This means the gut lining stops carrying out its role in protecting the body from bacteria, toxins, and undigested food particles. These pass through to the bloodstream, causing all the symptoms outlined above. I should caution you that there are still many doctors who deny the existence of leaky gut, despite increasing evidence to the contrary.[1]

THE CAUSES OF LEAKY GUT

It's unsurprising to learn that there are many foods that can damage your gut. These include:

Gluten

Modern wheat varieties contain much higher levels of gluten than in the past. In some sensitive people this gluten can be a major trigger. Gluten is found in grains like wheat, spelt, rye, and barley.[2]

Cutting out gluten from your diet can reverse the damage, giving your gut a chance to repair and the leaky openings to close.

Other grains

Some people find that if they react to gluten, they also have issues with seeds such as quinoa or buckwheat, common gluten substitutes. Try eliminating these from your diet for a few months before reintroducing them to see if your symptoms improve.

Lectins

Lectins are naturally occurring insecticides. Plants produce them to help combat pests. In your gut, the properties that make lectins so bad for insects and fungi can also damage your gut. Lectins are present in foods such as:

- Grains - wheat, rice, spelt, etc.
- Legumes - kidney beans, lentils, soy, etc.
- Peanuts
- Vegetables
- Fruits

If you've been experiencing problems with your digestive system, lowering your consumption of lectins is a good idea. At least, eliminate those foods highest in lectins, such as grains and legume. If you really must eat beans, soak them overnight and cook them well, which will reduce the amount of lectins they contain. Some people find that adding kombu, also known as kelp, when cooking legumes makes them more digestible.

Unsprouted grains, seeds, nuts, and beans

As well as containing lectins, these also contain chemicals such as phytates which inflame the digestive tract and block the absorption of nutrients by binding to essential minerals like calcium and magnesium. This can change the balance of gut bacteria.

Try soaking grains, seeds, and legumes overnight in lemon, apple cider vinegar, or salt to begin the sprouting process and lower the plant chemicals.

Dairy products

If you have a lactose intolerance, dairy will damage the gut. Research by Cornell University found that after childhood, at least

60% of adult's bodies will stop producing lactase, an essential enzyme for the digestion of milk.[4]

Processed meat products

These contain chemicals linked to cancer and inflammation, such as nitrates and nitrites.

Coffee

Even decaffeinated coffee can cause your gut to produce too much acid. Coffee can also irritate the stomach lining so it can't repair a leaky gut.

Antibiotics in food

Antibiotics can be found in the food chain. Just as taking antibiotics to treat a disease can upset the balance of gut flora, so too can antibiotics in food. Whenever possible, eat organic meat and wild-caught fish to avoid this.

Reactive foods

Everyone is different. What causes a reaction in one person is fine for another. This is why it's so important to listen to your body to identify what's an issue for you. In your Workbook, you'll be encouraged to pay more attention to your diet and what could be triggers for you.

The most common foods that cause gut problems are sugar, gluten, dairy, soy, eggs, and corn. Some people also have a problem with nightshades like eggplants and potatoes. Others have issues with FODMAPs. These are carbohydrates that cause unhealthy fermentation and encourage the growth of bad bacteria. Examples of these include barley, yogurt, apples, apricots, pears, and cauliflower.

OTHER CAUSES OF LEAKY GUT

While your diet has a lot to do with gut health, there are other potential triggers for leaky gut.

Chronic Constipation

If you suffer from ongoing constipation, this can change your gut flora, which may cause leaky gut and immune system reactions.[5]

If you want to know whether your gut is functioning properly, eat corn on the cob or take charcoal tablets. If it takes more than 24 hours for these to appear in your stool, you'll know that your gut transit time is slow.

Diarrhea

If you experience loose and sticky stool on a regular basis, this could be a sign your gut integrity is compromised.[6]

Proton Pump Inhibitor Medications (PPIs)

Taking PPIs for acid reflux might improve your symptoms on the surface, but they lower the normal acid balance in the stomach. Over time, rather than making things better, reduced stomach acid can cause inflammation, food sensitivities and other immune responses.

Other Medications

Many medications are known to cause gut problems. Non-steroidal anti-inflammatories like Ibuprofen are known to negatively affect the gut lining. Chronic use can cause stomach ulcers and bleeding. Even if you only take them once or twice a week, they may still cause inflammation. Antibiotics can also harm the gut, especially when taken frequently.

Infections

Problems such as Candida, h. Pylori, or parasite infections can all harm the gut.

HEALING YOUR LEAKY GUT

You've probably recognized the symptoms of leaky gut in yourself. Even if you feel that you don't have a problem, the process for healing your gut will help your burnout symptoms, so I would advise you to follow the protocol I'm about to give you to see the difference it makes.

Diet

While food can cause leaky gut, it can also heal it. Eliminating problem foods should give you immediate relief from your symptoms. While I would advise seeking medical supervision when cutting out food groups, as part of your 30-Day Program in your Workbook, you will be guided to start by removing gluten and dairy from your diet and see how you feel. You might like to start by cutting out dairy - if this is a problem food for you, you should experience improvements within a few days. Then remove gluten. It can take a little longer for gluten to leave the system (around three months) but again, you will still see improvements quickly.

If in doubt as to whether cutting out a food is making a difference, go for two weeks without it and then reintroduce it and see what happens.

Rotate your diet so you don't rely on the same foodstuffs. Many people develop a sensitivity when they eat the same foods all the time. Almonds and coconut are prime suspects for this.

A low glycaemic index (GI) diet with a wide range of fruit, vegetables, and fiber - the rainbow plate - can encourage a diverse gut microbiome. Cut out so-called white carbs like pasta, rice, and potatoes. This can trigger a rapid rise in blood sugar, eventually causing insulin resistance. This triggers inflammation in the body.

Try to keep at least 70% of your diet plant-based. Most people find cooked vegetables are better for them rather than raw (because this can help reduce lectins, etc.) but listen to your body and do what feels right for you. Cruciferous vegetables such as broccoli have compounds that ease the detoxification of estrogen.

Stop eating processed foods such as cereals, protein shakes, powders, puffed rice, and flours.

Cut back your alcohol consumption to one glass of wine two or three times a week or don't drink at all. Stay within the safe limits of 14 units of alcohol a week - a large glass of wine can contain 3 units.

Take digestive enzymes roughly half an hour before eating. This will help your body break down and absorb a wider range of nutrients.

Your gut biome has around 100 trillion different bacteria. Incredibly, we have 10 times more bacteria in our bodies than we do our own cells. When there are more 'bad' bacteria in your digestive system than 'good', this can cause inflammation, leading to leaky gut. Support your gut biome by taking pro- and prebiotics. You can take supplements if a therapeutic dose is needed. Prebiotics can be found in foods such as Jerusalem artichokes, garlic, onions, leeks, asparagus, bananas, barley, oats, and apples.

Eat fermented foods. These also have lots of good bacteria. You might like to try sauerkraut, lacto-fermented cucumbers, miso (if soy is tolerated), kefir, or kimchi. A word of caution - people suffering from digestive dysbiosis, Candida, or histamine intolerance don't do well with fermented food, so pay attention to your body's reactions to see if fermented food is right for you.

Have more resistant starch. Foods such as oats, lentils, bananas, cashews, and cooked, cooled potatoes have a fiber called resistant starch. This will go through your small intestine undigested and will only be absorbed when it reaches the colon. There it is fermented by the bacteria in the colon to produce short-chain fatty acids which help keep your gut healthy.

Filter your water to remove chemicals such as chlorine and fluoride which can kill the good bacteria in your gut.

Take supplements to heal your leaky gut. Possible options include:

- L-Glutamine, which repairs and seals the junctions between cells. It also promotes the production of glutathione, called 'the mother of antioxidants.' However, in some people, L-Glutamine can trigger anxiety when it is converted to glutamate, so if you find this makes your stress worse, not better, stop taking it. Start on a low dose to see whether it works for you before increasing the dosage.

- Slippery elm bark which creates a mucosal protection for the gut wall, bringing down inflammation and healing it.

- Curcumin which can bring down inflammation in the gut and elsewhere.

OTHER WAYS TO HEAL YOUR GUT

Avoid antibiotics unless absolutely necessary. Seek medical advice before taking antibiotics to ensure they are essential. Taking antibiotics as a matter of course to treat colds, viruses, or acne should be avoided since they take out all your gut bacteria, good and bad, which can cause lingering effects for years. Research has shown that six months after stopping antibiotics, most healthy people have recovered their normal microbiome composition and function. However, there can still be a lack of good bacteria, which is why pre- and probiotics can be so helpful.[9]

Be aware of your environment. There are many ways in which you can be exposed to estrogens, toxins, and heavy metals in the environment. Xenoestrogens are manufactured and used in common household products like fragrances, pesticides, and plastics. These are absorbed by the body and stored in the liver and fat cells. Here they can interact with naturally produced estrogens, upsetting your body's delicate hormone balance.

Carefully examine the products you buy and look for ways in which you can reduce your exposure to these toxic substances, replacing them with more environmentally friendly products. Try to lower your use of plastic as much as possible.

Physical activity naturally supports the detoxification process. Regular moderate intensity exercise can lower the amount of estrogens circulating through the body. It can also bring down cortisol levels.

Listen to your body and don't overdo it - too much exercise can be as harmful as too little. You might like to ease yourself into exercise with a gentle form of exercise such as yoga, which naturally stimulates the body's rest and digest mode. Practicing mindfulness can also help your body deal more effectively with stress and balance hormone levels.

Since diet is such an important part of healing your body and enjoying good physical and mental health in the future, we're going to examine it in further depth in the next chapter.

10

FEED, DON'T DEPRIVE

How To Consume A Diet Which Genuinely Supports Your Health

By choosing healthy over skinny you are choosing self-love over self-judgment.

– Steve Maraboli

I want to share a story with you about one of my clients which makes my point in a way that boring statistics never could.

When Devon came to see me, he told me that he had been suffering from chronic ill health for as long as he could remember. He was exhausted and struggling to find the energy to do anything these days. It had gotten so bad he'd recently been signed off work due to stress. He was fed up feeling this way and had come to me as a last resort. Doctors had only been able to paper over the cracks, not find a permanent solution.

It had started in his late 20s. He'd been suffering with stomach problems which he now thought were probably stress and diet related. In our initial discussion, it was soon apparent he was suffering from severe burnout which was particularly harming his gut. He had severe gastric reflux, so his doctor prescribed him Proton Pump Inhibitors. As you know from the last chapter, this can make things a lot worse in the long run.

When Devon told me how long he'd been taking PPIs, it was difficult for me to hide my shock. The packaging clearly states not to take them for longer than 6-8 weeks. Devon had been on them for 8 *years*, taking one every day during that time.

"If I don't take a pill, I get burning acid up in my throat," he told me. "I know they're not good for me, but what else can I do?"

"I have some ideas," I told him. "But tell me a little more about your current state of health."

"It seems like whenever I get one health issue sorted, something else comes up. I'm feeling more and more fatigued. I'm getting random pains in my joints. I've been getting breakouts on my skin, which is really annoying - I thought I left those back in high school!"

"And what have you done about that?"

"My doctor prescribed me various lotions and potions, but nothing really solved it. He did a few tests to try and figure out why I was so tired, but couldn't come up with an answer. In the end, he sent me to a consultant who decided I had discoid lupus. He told me it's a systemic immune system response to something going on in your body, but there's nothing you can do about it. All he could do was give me even more tablets."

"And is that what brought you here?"

Devon shook his head. "No. It was when my doctor did a cholesterol test a few weeks ago. The results came back - 7.0. He said it was a shocking result for someone my age and if I was obese or older, he'd put me on more drugs to bring it down. The thought of taking even more pills to paper over the cracks was a step too far. I started looking into my options. That's how I found you."

"I'm glad you did," I told him. "I think I can help you. The first step is to look at your diet."

Over the course of our sessions, we completely overhauled Devon's diet. We cut back on the amount of animal fat he was consuming and brought more variety into his diet. He started eating more oily fish, vegetables, fruit and nuts. He had a few meat-free days a week. He stopped drinking caffeinated drinks completely, increasing his water intake instead.

It wasn't long before Devon came into one of our sessions with a huge grin on his face.

"The doctor did another cholesterol test," he told me. "And guess what? It's dropped down to 5.3! I've still got a little way to go to get it under 5, but how incredible is that?"

"And how about the rest of your burnout symptoms?"

"I knew you could work miracles, but I didn't realize just how amazing your protocol was," Devon replied. "My skin's cleared up. I've stopped taking the PPIs because I don't need them. I get occasional heartburn if I eat something I shouldn't but I know what triggers it, so I can avoid it. I don't get pain in my joints anymore and my energy levels are through the roof. I can't remember when I last felt this good. In fact, I don't know if I've ever felt this great. I know it's easy to take a pill to reduce stomach acid, but those pills were doing more harm than good. We'd fix one issue but something else would spring up. Now I know that I can deal with the underlying cause. I've totally changed my lifestyle and I'm never going to go back."

While I can't promise you'll get the same results as Devon, I've seen similar changes in countless clients. If there's one thing I hope people take away from this book, it's that your diet really does affect every aspect of your life.

There's a few things I want you to be aware about. Not all body types are the same. There's no one specific diet that will be the magic pill to solve everything. As I mentioned in the previous chapter, you're going to have to play detective to figure out what foods are good for you and what ones aren't. You need to view all these changes as a lifestyle change rather than a fad diet you follow for 30 days then revert back to your old ways. If you want to see lasting, positive impact, you need to say goodbye to your old diet and welcome a completely new relationship with food.

MACRONUTRIENTS

When it comes to your diet, not all calories are created equal. Different body types respond differently to different foods due to your individual ability to use certain nutrients for fuel. This is why some nutritionists are moving away from keeping their focus solely on calories and instead count and track macronutrients to support wellbeing.

Macronutrients are nutrients we need in relatively large quantities to give our bodies energy and support bodily functions. There are three main types of macronutrients:

> **Carbohydrates** are the body's main source of energy. They're broken down into glucose before passing into the bloodstream. They support the nervous system, kidneys, brain, and muscles. Carbohydrates can be found in starchy foods such as bread, rice, potatoes, pasta, etc. Starchy carbohydrates with a higher fiber content, such as whole grain versions, release glucose into the blood slower than food and drink that are higher in sugar.
>
> **Protein** is required to build and maintain body tissues, such as muscles, as well as providing energy. Good sources of protein include meat, fish, eggs, soya products, nuts, and pulses.

Fats are necessary to maintain cell structures. They also carry fat-soluble vitamins like vitamins A, D, E, and K.

There are various different ways of counting your macros. Which version you use will depend on your individual requirements. I suggest starting by getting 50% of your calories from carbs, 30% from protein and 20% from fat and see how you feel. You can then adjust as you need, e.g. 40% carbs, 30% protein, 30% fat. If in doubt, consult a nutritionist. You could get them to put together an initial plan for you and then adjust it as you see fit as you become more in tune with your body's needs.

MICRONUTRIENTS

As well as getting the right balance of macronutrients, you'll also need to pay attention to your micronutrient intake. Micronutrients are those vitamins and minerals which are only needed in small amounts but allow the body to produce enzymes, hormones and other essential substances required for development, disease prevention and wellbeing.

There are 26 essential vitamins and minerals that play a vital role in countless bodily functions. Higher intakes of micros are associated with enhanced mood, elevated energy levels and appetite control.[1] Even if a deficiency is minor, correcting your micronutrient balance can have a dramatic impact on your health and day to day life.

Make sure you consume a broad range of nutrient dense whole (unprocessed) foods to increase your overall intake of micros. You might want to consider taking a high quality supplement as well. Eating a balanced, healthy diet will go a long way towards healing your gut and combating your burnout. It might take a little bit of research and tweaking to put together an appropriate meal plan which provides the right blend of macronutrients, but time invested now will pay dividends in the future. Eat at least five servings of colorful fruit and vegetables every day and mix up the types you consume to make sure you get a full range of natural vitamins and minerals. You might decide that taking a supplement is a good idea, at least at the start of this process to give your healing journey a boost so you can hit the ground running.

In the next chapter we're going to look at the domino effect. We're going to start bringing everything together so you can see how an imbalance in just one part of your system has a knock on effect, sending you into burnout. This will enable you to be more mindful about your life and take steps to head off burnout before it can take hold because you'll know how to identify the signs.

11

THE DOMINO EFFECT

Why A Holistic Approach Is The Only Way To Tackle Burnout

It was a domino effect... When you get one injury, that's when the other ones start coming.

– John Hall

"I thought I was doing okay," Joanne told me. "I mean, I was tired all the time, but I figured that's life. I was under a lot of pressure at work - there'd been a string of redundancies and those of us who'd kept our jobs were under pressure to perform. My daughter had just been diagnosed with autism and her school was no help, so it was like there was nowhere I could go to escape from stress. But that's what being a mother is all about. You're the one who has to hold it all together."

"That must have been hard for you," I said.

"It was," Joanne told me, "but I felt like I could stay on top of it if I just focused on putting one foot in front of the other. But then I started developing health problems. I was coming down with one bug after another, so I was having to take time off work. My manager was understanding at first, but after a while it became clear they were getting frustrated with me not being there when the team had been cut back due to the redundancies. I couldn't risk losing my job when I was having to pay for therapies for my daughter, so I tried to push through but I was rapidly going downhill. Then I started having problems with my digestion."

As if on cue, her stomach rumbled. She laughed, embarrassed.

"See what I mean?" Joanne said. "I've lost my appetite and I'm losing weight. I feel like I'm wasting away to nothing. Soon, there won't be any of me left."

I could tell she was fighting back tears.

"We won't let it get that far," I promised her. "You'll see. We'll start with doing a full analysis of your current situation and then we'll put together a plan to turn things around. I think you'll find that as you start seeing improvements in one part of your life, things will pick up across the board."

We've covered a lot of material so far about your physical and mental health and how imbalances in your various systems add up to burnout. Now it's time to look at how this domino effect really works because it affects *everything*. If one hormone is imbalanced, your entire hormonal system goes off kilter. If one organ isn't working properly, it affects your other systems. Your mental state affects your physical health. A positive outlook attracts positive experiences while a pessimistic one creates self-fulfilling prophecies.

And here's the best bit about this domino effect. While one thing going wrong can cause a cascade of negativity, an upward shift in one aspect of your life can create more positivity elsewhere. For example, if you're less stressed, you're calmer and respond to situations in a more reasoned manner so your relationships improve, you're more productive and life becomes better overall.

YOUR HORMONES

We've covered many of the areas underlying your burnout - mindset, reducing inflammation and supporting the body's natural detoxification system, and gut health. Now it's time to move on to the final piece of the puzzle: your hormones.

Your hormones are the body's chemical messengers. They send signals into the bloodstream and tissues to trigger specific processes. Hormones work slowly over time and affect numerous core processes, including growth, development, metabolism, sexual function, reproduction, and mood. When your body isn't producing the right amount of hormones, diseases can develop that affect many aspects of health.

Stress has a major effect on your hormones. Your body is hard-wired to react to stress in ways that are supposed to protect you, which is fine if you're suddenly faced with a saber-toothed tiger, but when you're under chronic pressure because of work, bills, family demands, etc. your body interprets these as being equally threatening and you can feel like you're permanently under attack.

When your body perceives you are under threat, your hypothalamus (a region of the brain located at its base) sets off an alarm system in your body. Nerves and hormones work together to make your adrenal glands flood the body with hormones including adrenaline and cortisol.

Adrenaline raises your heart rate, increases your blood pressure and increases the amount of energy available. Cortisol, the main stress hormone, increases the level of glucose in the bloodstream, makes the brain use more glucose and increases the amount of substances that repair tissues. It also limits functions that are nonessential or outright harmful in a fight-or-flight situation. It changes the immune system responses and suppresses the digestive system, the reproductive system, and growth processes. In addition, this natural response triggers the brain regions controlling mood, motivation, and fear.

This stress response system usually shuts itself off once the threat has passed. As adrenaline and cortisol levels drop, so does your heart rate and blood pressure, while your other systems return to normal. Or at least, that's how it's supposed to work. When you feel like you're constantly under attack due to stress, this fight-or-flight response stays activated and doesn't switch off. This increases your risk of suffering any or all of the health problems associated with burnout.

A HEALTHY HORMONAL SYSTEM

When your hormones are balanced, you feel great. Rather than feeling burnt out, you experience a range of positive symptoms, including:

- Your energy levels are regulated, elevated, and predictable. As evening approaches and you prepare for sleep, your energy levels slowly fall.

- You wake up feeling refreshed.

- You find it easy to fall asleep within 15 minutes of settling down and have no problem staying asleep. If you need to get up to urinate, you don't have any problems falling back asleep.

- You have regular bowel movements (at least once a day). Stools are log shaped, not sticky and easy to pass. You only need to wipe yourself a couple of times to clean afterwards. There's no sensation of any leftover stool in the colon or rectum once you're done.

- You don't experience any bloating, gas, cramps, or acid reflux during the day.

- Your mood is balanced and predictable with no unexplained mood swings.

- You don't have any aches or pains in your joints or muscles. You are physically mobile, light, and agile.

- You don't suffer from brain fog. Your mind is clear and you can think straight.

- You don't have any headaches.

- You don't have any difficulty with breathing when you're at rest or with carrying out light activities such as walking or going up and down satire.

- You have a healthy appetite so you don't have any specific cravings for certain foods or flavors after having regular programmed meals. You don't get any unusual cravings in comparison to what would be "usual" for you.

- Your urine is light straw colored. You don't experience pain when you urinate and you don't have any issues with passing urine.

- You are fully hydrated throughout the day. You do not suffer from a dry mouth, dry lips or thirst.

- You do not have any rashes, itchiness or atypical skin symptoms.

This is the ultimate goal for all the work you're doing to heal your burnout. While you should have seen a lot of progress if you've been keeping up with the program, there's still more work to be done to balance your metabolism and improve your health.

HOW STRESS CAUSES THYROID PROBLEMS

There is a link between thyroid and stress. Thyroid hormones are connected to the body's natural stress systems and stress hormones such as cortisol. This means that if you have thyroid issues, you could be more sensitive to stress.

People with hypothyroidism (when the thyroid doesn't produce enough thyroid hormones) or hyperthyroidism (when the thyroid produces too much thyroid hormones) often question whether stress caused their illness or is making their symptoms worse. The jury is out on this one with a lack of research, but my personal experience would suggest that given the impact of stress on health, there is a good chance that stress at least makes thyroid issues worse and there are some studies to support this theory.[1]

Excessively high or low levels of thyroid hormones impact how the body's stress responses work. Stress stimulates the production of cortisol, which can inhibit the secretion of TSH. This in turn can limit the production of thyroxine, the main hormone created by the thyroid gland. So you can end up in a downward spiral, where stress worsens the symptoms of thyroid disease, causing more stress.

YOUR NEW HEALTHY HABITS

All the work you've been doing so far has been designed to work in a systematic fashion to undo the damage caused by stress which has resulted in your burnout. In your Workbook, you'll find exercises which build on the foundations you've laid, working in all the areas that need to be supported to heal the damage.

Remember, it's important to watch the quality of your thoughts. While it's only natural to have negative thoughts when dealing with difficult situations, remember that you are not your thoughts. You can always take a moment to step back, examine your thoughts, and question whether they're true.

Pay Attention To Your Diet

The key to your physical and mental health. If you're eating throughout the day, consider giving your gut a break. You've probably heard of intermittent fasting and the "structuredness" of it. But it doesn't have to be strict like that, especially for females who are still menstruating. The foundational purpose of intermittent fasting is to allow your body to be more efficient with its fuel usage and give your gut the opportunity to rest. If you're a female, your fasting time throughout the month should be synced to your cycle. Here are some ways to structure your daily fasting times.

> **Alternate-day fasting.** This is when you eat a normal diet one day and follow it with a day when you either totally fast or only eat one small meal of less than 500 calories.
>
> **5:2 fasting.** This is when you eat normally five days a week and fast for the other two.
>
> **Daily time-restricted fasting.** This is when you eat normally within an eight-hour window. For example, you might not have breakfast, but eat lunch at midday and have your dinner before 8pm.

This is often suggested as a good way of losing weight, but there is some research to show that intermittent fasting can reduce inflammation and help heal other symptoms associated with burnout.[2]

Sweat

In your Workbook, you've been encouraged to do exercise which makes you sweat for increasing periods of time. Moving your body will help stimulate the feel-good hormones required to counter the stress-inducing hormones. Choose a form of exercise which you enjoy and which appeals to you. If you like an activity, you're more likely to feel motivated to stick with it. You could go to the gym, join a local outdoor running club, go for a swim - if you're feeling really brave, you might like to try wild swimming in lakes and rivers - dance, do a martial art, etc. etc. The possibilities are endless.

It really doesn't matter what you choose. Anything will work as long as it raises your heart rate and gets you active.

Clean Up Your Environment

You may be surprised by how many hormone-disrupting chemicals are in your home, contributing to your burnout. Here's some simple ways you can start:

- Wash your hands frequently throughout the day. (Avoid fragranced or antibacterial soap.) Always wash before eating and after using the bathroom. You'll eliminate a lot of chemical residue this way.

- Regularly dust and vacuum. Despite being linked to cancer and hormone disruption, flame retardant chemicals are used in many household products. These chemicals escape from electronics, couches, and baby products, ending up in dust in your home. You may not have the budget to replace everything with flame-retardant-free versions, but frequently dusting with a damp cloth and using a vacuum with a HEPA filter will minimize your exposure to dust and chemicals such as lead, phthalates, and fluorinated chemicals.

- Choose fragrance free products. Companies do not have to declare the ingredients in their fragrances. Phthalates are often used in fragrances and are known to disrupt hormones. If you want to freshen up your home, open windows, use fans and remove sources of bad smells, such as trash and used cat litter instead of trying to cover them up. You can also use natural fragrances such as fresh flowers in the kitchen, citrus peels in the garbage disposal or keeping an open box of baking soda in the fridge.

- Reduce your use of plastics as much as possible. While it's almost impossible to avoid, many plastics contain hormone-disrupting chemicals. Even small exposures to these chemicals can be problematic.[3] Use glass or stainless steel containers instead of plastic ones. Replace plastic baggies with reusable lunch bags and swap plastic cling wrap for beeswax coated cloth. Give your children toys made from natural materials, such as wood and cotton, instead of plastic. Whenever you have the option, go for a plastic-free alternative.

- Avoid cans. While canned foods are convenient, they may well be lined with BPA to prevent corrosion. Even if marked

BPA-free, they may contain similar chemicals which have not been proven to be safer. Go for fresh, frozen, or dried food instead of cans.

- Eat organic as much as possible and go for whole foods. If you can, avoid food packaging. Look at what you use to prepare food as well. Nonstick pots and pans can also have nasty chemicals, so use stainless steel or cast iron ones instead.

- Filter your tap water. While drinking out of a glass will lower your exposure to BPAs and chemicals found in cans and plastic bottles, tap water can also contain other hormone disruptors, such as residue from birth control pills. If you get an NSF-certified water filter installed properly, this will lower the amount of endocrine-disrupting chemicals in the water.

- Don't use cosmetics on your kids. While there are plenty of products marketed to children, they can contain many EDCs and other chemicals linked to cancer, asthma, and skin irritation. If you want to use lotions, sunscreens, and soap, check the product on the Environmental Working Group's database at https://www.ewg.org/skindeep to find ones which have a minimum of nasties.

- Make your own cleaning products, look for ones which have the Safer Choice label, or buy from companies that list out their ingredients. Dilute white vinegar and baking soda are both effective cleaners without the nasty side effects. Using natural products or ones which are free from nasty chemicals will prevent you inadvertently bringing pollutants into your home.

LIMIT THE AMOUNT OF STRESS IN YOUR LIFE

Yes. Easier said than done. But as you know, stress is linked to serious health conditions - including burnout. The more you can do to reduce the levels of stress you're under, the more you'll support yourself to recover from burnout.

Stress comes at us from many directions. Take time to assess your life and look at what you can do to reduce your stress levels.

Examine your finances. Financial stress is one of the greatest problems most of us deal with. Get financial advice if you need help with budgeting. You may well find that there are local charities which provide these services for free. Talk to people about your money problems - you may be surprised to find how understanding companies can be, especially after Covid had such an impact on so many people's livelihood.

Think about your career. Exercises you've done in previous chapters helped you to define your ideal life. Is your current career part of that picture? Does it support your plans for the future? If not, it may be time to start making some bold decisions about change.

Build a support network. Surrounding yourself with people who support your new, healthy approach to life will help you maintain your positive habits. If you struggle with making connections, you could always start by joining a few online groups and reach out there to build up your confidence before looking at local, in-person options.

Reading about making changes for the rest of your life may seem daunting or overwhelming. But when you actually do them, you'll discover it's a very different matter. It's fun! The program in this book has been designed to gradually put you on the right path without you even realizing. All you're doing is continuing the good work.

Now you have all the knowledge you need to never feel burnt out again. You know what causes burnout. This means you'll be able to spot the signs if you start backsliding.

But you're not going to do that, are you?

Because now you're living a life free of burnout. Why would you ever want to go back? Remember: it's your life and you're in control. Which leads me to ...

CONCLUSION

It's A Lifestyle And You're In Control

"Can I tell you something silly?" Lisa asked. We'd been working together for a while and this was our last session together.

"You can tell me anything. You know that." I smiled warmly to reassure her.

"You've helped me so much. I never thought I could feel like this again. If anything, I feel better than I ever have. It's like recovering from my burnout has helped me go up to the next level."

"There's nothing silly about that."

"No, that's not the silly part." Lisa shook her head. "I'm worried that my burnout will come back. I feel so good I'm terrified I'll go back to being burnt out again."

"There's nothing silly about that either," I reassured her. "It's really common to feel afraid of going back there. But the first thing to remember is mindset - focus on how you want to feel, not how you *don't* want to feel. You have your roadmap for what to do. Everything we've done has been geared towards making a lifelong lifestyle change. Keep doing what you've been doing and you'll never have to worry about burnout again."

It's true. All the changes I've guided you through in this book aren't a plaster or a quick fix. They're permanent, lifelong changes which will allow you to enjoy abundant energy and good health moving forward.

Look at it this way - doing what you did before got you into burnout. Doing what you're doing now got you out of it. If you don't want to slide back into burnout, keep doing what you're doing!

You started on this journey because you knew something needed to change. Look back at the vision you set for your ideal life when you first started on this process. You imagined how it would feel to have boundless energy, doing work you love, surrounded by positive people who support you and celebrate your success. If you've been following the program, you won't need to imagine it anymore. You'll start to see real evidence of it in your life.

If not, go back over the process to see what step(s) you're neglecting. Does your mindset need work? Are you prioritizing the right things? Re-examine the process and see where you can give more attention to get the results you want.

You can also seek support and find more information in the LearnWell Community.

Here's the thing. You're sick and tired of feeling sick and tired. It feels like there's no way out and nothing can change. But it *can* change. You have the power to turn things around and it's never too late.

Before we finish, let's review some of the key points I've shared with you so that they remain at the front of your mind.

MINDSET

Take time every day to sit with that feeling you had while you were visualizing your ideal self. Your subconscious can't tell the difference between reality and imagination, so the more you fill your mind with these positive feelings, the easier it will be to move forward.

Focus on the daily tasks detailed in your Workbook. Forget about the rate of progress. Just do the little things you have to do every day. This work will soon pay off.

Be present as much as you can. Leave the past behind you and let the future come when it does. All you have is this present moment, so savor it.

Identify your limiting beliefs and challenge them. Actively reprogram them so you can have the life you want. Use your Workbook to make note of your limiting beliefs. Then determine where those beliefs came from. Understand the underlying limiting belief and decide whether it's really true. (It's not.) Change the limiting belief to one which supports the lifestyle you aspire to.

Start establishing healthy habits to replace the negative ones which got you to this place.

REDUCING INFLAMMATION AND SUPPORTING DETOXIFICATION

Support the body's natural detox system. Increase your water intake and start eating more fruit and vegetables. Keep the focus on adding in new, healthy wholefoods rather than thinking about what you can't have anymore. You can eat what you want. But you're now choosing to consume more of the foods which nourish your body rather than the ones which feed your burnout.

GUT HEALTH

Your gut has an essential role to play in your overall health and wellbeing. Stress can overwhelm your digestive system, causing abdominal pain and other issues. Likewise, problems with your gut can increase anxiety and stress.

Improving your diet will go a long way towards healing your gut. Eliminating problem foods will quickly improve your symptoms. Filter your water to remove harmful chemicals and consider taking supplements to support gut health.

As well as cleaning your diet, clean your environment. There are many products in the environment which contain damaging chemicals. The more you can avoid these products, the easier it will be for your gut to heal.

HORMONES AND YOUR METABOLISM

Your hormones are another essential key to health. When you're under chronic stress, the body's production of adrenaline and cortisol goes into overdrive, flooding your body with these stress hormones on an ongoing basis.

As well as your hormones, your metabolism plays a major part in maintaining health.

Both your hormones and metabolism require appropriate nutrients to function properly. Eat whole foods to nourish your body and avoid processed foods as much as you can. Consider intermittent fasting to support your hormones and metabolism and reduce inflammation.

Follow your body's natural rhythms. Your body will always gravitate towards a state of health where possible. Working with your body rather than against it will make it easier for you to heal.

Reduce sources of stress as much as possible. Where there are areas you don't feel you can change at the moment, such as your job, or relationships with certain people, the more you can do to cut stress from your life, the more you can cope with the remaining stressors.

Above all, consider this: if you truly want to escape your burnout, you're going to have to make some changes. Doing what you've always done got you to this place. You'll need to commit to making lifestyle changes which you maintain for the rest of your life. It'll be worth it. I promise.

And be kind to yourself. Take one step at a time and eventually you'll get to where you want to be.

Thank you for taking this journey with me. I'm grateful for you and the trust you've placed in me. I truly hope it will set you free of the burnout that was limiting your potential.

Wishing you good health and the live you deserve,

Dr. Deanna Rose

x

REFERENCES

Introduction

1. 1 https://www.forbes.com/sites/jackkelly/2021/04/05/indeed-study-shows-that-worker-burnout-is-at-frighteningly-high-levels-here-is-what-you-need-to-do-now/

Chapter One

1. https://theconversation.com/explainer-how-do-you-die-from-overwork-18023
2. https://www.mind.org.uk/information-support/tips-for-everyday-living/nature-and-mental-health/how-nature-benefits-mental-health/
3. https://www.bbc.com/worklife/article/20190312-the-tiny-breaks-that-ease-your-body-and-reboot-your-brain
4. https://www.work-fit.com/blog/how-effective-breaks-at-work-increase-productivity
5. https://www.helpguide.org/articles/diets/mindful-eating.htm
6. https://www.starlingminds.com/what-is-online-cognitive-behavioral-therapy-cbt-starling-minds/

Chapter Five

1. https://www.frontiersin.org/articles/10.3389/fmicb.2019.03067/full#:~:text=Repeated%20exposure%20to%20social%20stress,2014%3B%20Stilling%20et%20al.%2C

2. https://www.sciencedirect.com/science/article/pii/S0165032722001732
3. https://www.tandfonline.com/doi/full/10.3109/10253890.2011.606341
4. https://nutritionandmetabolism.biomedcentral.com/articles/10.1186/s12986-020-00513-4
5. https://www.scientificamerican.com/article/what-is-the-function-of-t-1997-12-22/

Chapter Six

1. https://web.colby.edu/cogblog/2020/11/24/moving-from-autopilot-towards-mindfulness/

Chapter Seven

1. https://www.ncbi.nlm.nih.gov/pmc/articles/PMC5476783/
2. https://www.nature.com/articles/mp2015168/
3. https://www.scientificamerican.com/article/can-visualizing-your-body-doing-something-help-you-learn-to-do-it-better/

Chapter Eight

1. https://onlinelibrary.wiley.com/doi/full/10.1046/j.1440-1746.2003.03032.x
2. https://www.ncbi.nlm.nih.gov/pmc/articles/PMC3384703/
3. https://news.cornell.edu/stories/2005/06/lactose-intolerance-linked-ancestral-struggles-climate-diseases
4. https://www.sciencedaily.com/releases/2014/05/140515132212.htm
5. https://www.medscape.com/viewarticle/535694_1

References

6. https://www.sciencedaily.com/releases/2018/10/181023110545.htm#:~:text=Summary%3A,nine%20common%20beneficial%20bacterial%20species.

Chapter Nine

1. https://nutritionj.biomedcentral.com/articles/10.1186/1475-2891-9-51

Chapter Ten

1. https://www.imaware.health/blog/stress-and-thyroid#:~:text=%22Stress%20increases%20production%20of%20the,Guandalini%20explains.
2. https://www.cell.com/cell/fulltext/S0092-8674(19)30850-5
3. https://www.ncbi.nlm.nih.gov/pmc/articles/PMC1280330/

www.ingramcontent.com/pod-product-compliance
Lightning Source LLC
Chambersburg PA
CBHW030220100526
44584CB00014BA/1396